The Launceston Branch

by
G.H. Anthony MCIT

Revised and Extended
by
Stanley C. Jenkins MA

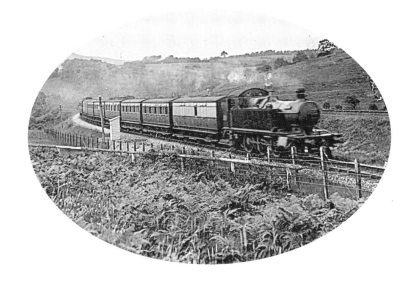

THE OAKWOOD PRESS

Incorporating material first published as *The Tavistock, Launceston & Princetown Railways* in 1971, reprinted 1983.

© Oakwood Press and S.C. Jenkins 1997

British Library Cataloguing in Publication Data
A Record for this book is available from the British Library
ISBN 0 85361 491 1

Typeset by Oakwood Graphics.
Repro by Ford Graphics, Ringwood, Hants.
Printed by Witney Press, Witney, Oxon.

The north end of Lifton station with 0-6-0PT No. 4679 arriving with a train from Launceston, 9th July, 1960. The arch that can be seen in the distance once carried a narrow gauge line to Tinhay Quarry. *Hugh Davies*

Front cover: A postcard view of Yelverton station around the turn of the century.
P. Strong Collection

Title page: '45XX' class 2-6-2T No. 4551 is seen near Mary Tavy on a Plymouth train in 1929. *C.E.W. Neat*

Published by
The Oakwood Press
P.O. Box 122, Headington, Oxford OX3 8LU

Contents

Gt Western Ry   Gt Western Ry
Plym'th N.Rd   Plym'th N. Rd
TO
MARY TAVY & BLACKDOWN
Via Marsh Mills.
THIRD CLASS
3/7   P   Fare 3/7   P
MaryTavy&B'do   MaryTavy&B'down
FOR CONDITI'   SEE BACK A.I.

A GWR 3rd class single ticket.   *John Strange Collection*

Introduction

Running for over thirty miles through remote, and sometimes beautiful Devonshire countryside, the line from Plymouth to Launceston was one of the Great Western's longer rural branch lines. The history of this line was surprisingly complex; the story really begins as far back as 1819 when a company known as the Plymouth & Dartmoor Railway was authorised to begin construction of a tramway from Plymouth to Princetown. A few years later, the South Devon & Tavistock Railway was promoted to build a line running more or less parallel to the original tramway as far as Yelverton, while in the 1860s a further company known as the Launceston & South Devon Railway was formed to extend the South Devon & Tavistock line to the town of Launceston.

This was by no means the end of the story, and in the next few years an entirely separate company - the Devon & Cornwall Railway - obtained Parliamentary consent to build a line from Okehampton to Lydford, at which point the existing Tavistock line provided a southwards route to Plymouth; the Devon & Cornwall Railway subsequently became part of the London & South Western Railway, and from 1879 until 1890 LSWR trains worked over the southern part of the Launceston branch. Meanwhile, in 1878, the Princetown Railway was incorporated with Powers to build a branch line from Yelverton to Princetown, using the route of the Plymouth & Dartmoor Railway for this purpose.

The story of the Launceston branch is, therefore, the history of at least five separate undertakings, all of which contributed, in one way or another, to the final branch line from Plymouth to Yelverton, Tavistock and Launceston.

The complicated history of the Launceston branch was recounted by G.H. Anthony in an Oakwood Press publication entitled *The Tavistock, Launceston & Princetown Railways*, which was first published in 1971 and reprinted in 1983. Although most readers were probably unaware of it at the time, George Anthony was himself a part of West Country railway history; a Cornishman, Mr Anthony had served at Helston and other GWR stations during the course of a long career on the Great Western Railway. In 1941 he went to Plymouth, where he had the distinction of becoming the last station master at Plymouth North Road. Born at the end of the 19th century, Mr Anthony was old enough to have known the Great Western Railway in its prime, and it follows that his history of the Launceston branch was a valuable source of historical evidence in its own right.

When asked to upgrade and expand Mr Anthony's original publication, I was conscious of the value of his original work, but at the same time it appeared to me that there was scope for a much-expanded 'route' section. I have, accordingly, retained most of Mr Anthony's text, but the chapter plan has been slightly modified to make room for the two greatly enlarged 'route' sections. Elsewhere, the text has been updated, expanded or clarified where necessary, while numerous new illustrations have been added to the original selection of maps and photographs.

A new title - *The Launceston Branch* - has been adopted in place of the somewhat cumbersome title formerly used. However, for the reasons stated above, any history of the Launceston route must inevitably encompass the Tavistock, Launceston *and* Princetown railways, and it is hoped that modern readers will appreciate this new version of George Anthony's work. It is also hoped that the late Mr Anthony would have approved of the transformation, and that, if he had lived long enough to rewrite his own book, he would have produced something not so very different from the present volume.

Stanley C. Jenkins
Witney, 1996

A postcard view of Launceston castle, showing the keep during the early 1900s.
English Heritage (South Western Museums Service)

Chapter One

The First Stages (1840-42)

Built in stages by two separate companies, the Launceston branch of the Great Western Railway was really *two* branch lines placed end to end. The southern portion of the route, from Plymouth to Tavistock, was promoted in the 1850s by the South Devon & Tavistock Railway, while the northern section of line from Tavistock to Launceston was constructed and opened in the following decade by the Launceston & South Devon Railway. Both companies nevertheless had a long pre-history - indeed railway development in the Dartmoor area commenced as long ago as the 1820s, when the influential landowner Thomas Tyrwhitt obtained Powers for construction of the pioneering Plymouth & Dartmoor Railway. The full story of this early line will be told in *Chapter Nine*, and the present chapter will therefore concern itself with the pre-history of the South Devon & Tavistock Railway.

Early Railway Schemes

Although railway communication with Tavistock was not secured until 22nd June, 1859, many schemes were brought before the public in the previous quarter of a century.

This was a period of great industrial development. The newly born railway, with all its teething troubles, was growing rapidly, and by extending its influence was bringing home to people the inescapable fact that if they wished to join in the increasing prosperity, rapid means of communication were essential to commercial well-being, and indeed, to economic existence.

The prospects were exciting, the rewards appeared to be very great. All classes of the community - whether they agreed or disagreed with the latest developments - were caught up in the struggle. Landowners looked upon railways with mixed feelings; the professional classes realised there would be a huge demand for the services of surveyors and engineers; lawyers would reap a rich harvest; engineering firms and manufacturers would prosper; steel works and coal mines would be inundated with orders. The working class would find plenty of hard work and, even if the pay was poor and conditions harsh, there would be no fear of unemployment. The middle class would be attracted by the high dividends on capital investment - so optimistically promised by the promoters - and those with leisure and means would be able to travel greater distances, at higher speeds, relatively low cost and increased comfort.

There was a surge of optimism throughout the country. Most people regarded the new order as exciting and challenging - the future certainly looked very rosy. It is a part of human nature to be optimistic, and the inevitable reaction, which brought disappointment, frustration and exploitation to some, could not be foreseen, neither could the breaking up of friendships and the destruction of loyalties which many were to experience in later years, when local opposition schemes were launched, and fierce arguments raged as to the merits or otherwise of particular schemes.

The people of Tavistock and district were to experience all the emotive forces released by progress, which embraced the best and the worst in human nature. The story of the town's efforts to secure a railway, which at first seemed so easy of accomplishment, was spread over a period of twenty years, and is one of fascination, hope, fear and frustration, but ultimately of accomplishment. To the railway enthusiast and local historian alike it is one of intense interest.

It was in the 1830s that interest was aroused in the coming of the railway in the area to the south and west of Dartmoor. The Great Western Railway, so prophetically and truly named, which was destined to have such a profound influence throughout the West Country, was incorporated on 31st August, 1835. Within a few weeks a prospectus of the Bristol & Exeter Railway was issued; there was little opposition to the Bristol & Exeter Bill, which became law on 19th May, 1836.

These developments were closely watched in the west, and a survey for a line from Plymouth to Exeter was made by Brunel in 1836, but the scheme fell through because of lack of financial backing.

In the meantime, the claims of Tavistock were not being overlooked. Francis Giles, the original Engineer of the London & Southampton Railway, proposed a line to the north of Dartmoor via Crediton and Okehampton to Tavistock. Although the scheme was supported by Exonians, the people of Plymouth withheld their support as they were considering a line of their own from Plymouth and Devonport to Exeter.

The Role of James Meadows Rendel

In the meantime a great deal of local activity had been going on; James Meadows Rendel (1799-1856) was a typical product of the Industrial Revolution. Apprenticed to Thomas Telford (1757-1834) the great road-builder and canal engineer, J.M. Rendel had first settled in Plymouth in the 1820s, where he became consulting engineer to Lord Morley and built the Lary Bridge, which was opened on 14th July, 1827. He was also Engineer to Johnson Brothers - the ostensible owners of the Plymouth & Dartmoor Railway, and later, in 1844, he became a member of the Committee of Management of that pioneering line.

About 1833, Rendel, who had a wide knowledge of Dartmoor, commenced a long study and series of investigations - carried out over a period of seven years - into railway communications between Plymouth and Exeter via Dartmoor, with a branch line from near Meavy to Tavistock. This led to a survey by H. Beardmore, under Rendel's direction, and to plans being deposited on 20th February, 1840 with the Clerk of the Peace for the County of Devon.

A 'Report of a proposed line of Railway, from Plymouth, Devonport and Stonehouse to Exeter, over the Forest of Dartmoor, with a branch line to Tavistock, by James M. Rendel, Civil Engineer, dated August 1840,' published by R. White Stevens of Plymouth, was considered on 28th October, 1840 at what was described as 'probably the most important meeting held in Plymouth in living memory.' Held in the Royal Hotel, it was presided over by the Mayor, Dr Cookworthy, who was supported by the Earl of Devon, Sir Ralph Lopes MP, representatives of the Duchy of Cornwall and the Duke of Bedford, T. Bewes Esq., MP for Plymouth, and J. Rundle Esq., MP for Tavistock, and was largely attended by members of the civic, commercial, and professional community.

In his report, Rendel stated:

> For many years it had been considered that Plymouth, Devonport, Stonehouse and Stoke, with a population of over 100,000 should be connected by rail with Exeter, there to connect with the proposed railway to Bath, and thence to the Metropolis.

In the delightful, if, to us, somewhat archaic phraseology of the time:

> It was felt that the lack of such a facility could not be imagined, as it is incompatible with the law of defence. If the people of Plymouth chose to remain in an isolated state compared with the rest of the kingdom, and were to be content with their present commerce and prosperity, they would soon discover that amidst so mighty a rivalship, there must follow a retrogradation from their actual importance until they dwindled into insignificance.

It was seen as a matter of national, as well as local importance, that Plymouth should be connected with London by a railway - thereby bringing its military and naval establishments into closer union with the controlling Board in London. Similar establishments were being brought within four hours journey of the 'Admiralty, the Horse Guards and the Ordnance' by the completion of the London & Southampton Railway, which gave Portsmouth a considerable advantage over Plymouth.

To bring Plymouth within ten hours, or in an emergency, seven hours of London, the greater natural advantage of Plymouth over Portsmouth, or any other harbour in the kingdom, would more than compensate for its greater distance.

In considering the general scheme it was considered important to include Tavistock. A branch line to that town from near Meavy would not only serve a large agricultural and mining district, but would provide a direct route to the centre of the county and connect the adjoining parts of Cornwall and North Devon. Tavistock would thus be brought within 14 miles of Plymouth and 41 miles of Exeter.

Some Details of Rendel's Scheme

James Rendel's initial surveys had covered three possible routes, the overall bearing being a straight line running roughly north-east to south-west from Exeter to Plymouth. The total distance, in each case, would be about 50 miles, although there was considerable variation between the three routes. In general, the possible routes were as follows.

(i) A survey to the north of Dartmoor via Okehampton involved a line of about 24 miles up the Tamar valley to Launceston, which place would be still 40 miles distant from Exeter, and would involve heavy engineering difficulties.

(ii) A route to the south of Dartmoor through the South Hams, already surveyed by Brunel in 1836, was again surveyed through Ivybridge, Totnes and Teignmouth, a total distance of 50 miles from Plymouth to Exeter. This involved inclined planes, tunnelling up to a total length of 2¼ miles, and would cost £30,000 per mile and a total estimated cost of £1,800,000.

(iii) The direct line from Plymouth to Exeter across Dartmoor would involve many river crossings, but the valleys would be easy and inexpensive to work. It would be 42¾ miles long, and its estimated cost would be £674,138. The Tavistock line would be five miles 1,000 yards long. Its estimated cost was £96,643, giving a total for the whole line of £770,781, a saving of over one million pounds as compared with the South Hams line.

The estimated cost of working the direct Plymouth to Exeter line, including the Tavistock portion, was £48,000, or £10,900 less than the estimated cost of working the South Hams line.

The line over Dartmoor would consist of one inclined plane worked by water-wheels, and only 21 miles worked by locomotives.

The direct line would commence close to Pennycomequick, proceed up the Houndiscombe Valley, cross the Devonport Road near Manadon then continue westwards to Knackersknowle on the Tavistock Road to Jump, where by means of deep cuttings it would drop into the valley of the Plym and on to Yelverton, passing through a tunnel onto the Walkham valley near Horrabridge to Wheal Franco mine, thence across a river and over a ridge of higher ground east of Grenofen into the Whitchurch valley; then to Tavistock, terminating in a field near the turnpike gate at the back of the Bedford Arms Hotel.

There would be a tunnel near Yelverton (1170 yards) and one (250 yards) between the third and fourth mileposts on the branch. The gradients on the southern section of line between Plymouth, Yelverton and Tavistock would be as shown in the following table:

Section of Line	*Gradient*	*Distance*	
		Miles	*Yards*
Pennycomequick to Knackersknowle	1 in 33 rising	1	1190
(worked by two stationary engines each of 60 hp)			
Knackersknowle to Yelverton	1 in 176 rising	6	528
Yelverton to Tavistock	⎧ 1 in 176 rising		
(worked by locomotives)	⎨ 1 in 132 falling	5	1000
Total		13	958

The route north-eastwards to Exeter from the junction with the Tavistock branch would be: Yelverton to Nun's Cross, then across the Forest to New House Pass, thence to Chagford and on to Exeter via the Perridge or Ide Valley. There would be tunnels at Nun's Cross (1300 yards) and New House Pass (1760 yards).

The distances were: Plymouth to Yelverton 7 miles 1718 yds, Tavistock Branch 5 miles 1000 yds, Yelverton to Exeter 34 miles 1304 yds - the total distance being 48 miles 502 yds.

Up trains would be brought from Plymouth to Knackersknowle by a rope attached to two fixed engines, then attached to a locomotive and taken to Yelverton, the Tavistock portion proceeding behind an engine while the Exeter portion would be attached to the plane rope and drawn by water-wheel to Nun's Cross station, where a locomotive would be attached for the journey across the Forest to New House Pass. From the latter station the train would be drawn by rope and water-wheel up the inclined plane to Chagford, from which point a locomotive would take over for the remaining 14 miles 44 yards to Exeter.

Trains would start from either terminus at the same time and would always meet on the Forest portion of the line between Nun's Cross and New House Pass (which would be a double line). There would be eight trains a day in each direction for which nine locomotives would be required. Allowing for relief engines and for an assisting engine on the Chagford-Exeter section, the stud of engines would be 14.

Up fast (or first) trains would have a speed of 18 mph with stoppages; down fast trains, with stoppages, would have a speed of 16 mph. The water-wheels would be capable of drawing trains up the inclines at speeds of 15 to 20 miles per hour.

Three dams would be built across river gorges to create reservoirs covering an area of 255 acres, with an average depth of 20 ft. The depth of water would be sufficient during a drought to pass eight trains a day up the plane for three months. They would be from 50 to 300 ft above the water-wheels which would allow the water to descend without the chance of being impeded either by frost or snow. The wheels would be underground or in chambers to protect them from severe winter conditions.

An Edwardian postcard view of Clapper Bridge, Dartmeet.
English Heritage (South Western Museums Service)

Resolutions were passed accepting the report, urging the making of the line from Plymouth to Tavistock and Exeter, with branches from Tavistock into the north of Devon and Cornwall, and appointing a Committee. Subscription lists would be opened inviting application for shares of £50 each, and when £50,000 had been subscribed provisional Directors would be appointed to give effect to the resolutions and to carry out the formation of the line as proposed.

The Committee met on 14th November, 1840 when it was reported that the share lists totalled £50,000. By 2nd December, 1840, the amount had increased to £62,000; provisional Directors were then appointed and it was resolved to present a Bill in the next session of Parliament.

By January 1841, however, doubts were being expressed about the entire scheme. It was felt that the terminal station at Plymouth was too far from the town centre, that the best financial return would not be secured by taking a line over Dartmoor's barren wastes (the Plymouth & Dartmoor Railway had already exposed this weakness) and it was very doubtful if the anticipated profit would be realised. A line near large centres of population, with a greater traffic potential, would be a better proposition.

These doubts took effect, and on 1st April, 1841, Mr McNeil, a civil engineer, was selected to survey the lines already proposed. He commenced his survey in the South Hams, first surveyed by Brunel in 1836.

Public support from Plymouth for the Dartmoor scheme continued to be lukewarm and at a meeting held at Exeter on 16th February, 1842 it was decided not to proceed further with the matter, 'as it is now apparent that the public will prefer the more lucrative line south of the Moor', which, at this date might refer either to McNeil's route via the South Hams or the Exeter, Plymouth & Devonport Railway (later known as the South Devon Railway) both of which were being surveyed and/or promoted at that time.

So ended James Rendel's dream of a line across Dartmoor. His plans had displayed great engineering ability and were in keeping with his great professional reputation. Rendel supplied details for another line from Tavistock to Plymouth, doubtless based upon his survey of 1840, which formed the basis of a prospectus issued in 1844 and will be referred to later.

Another line to Tavistock was proposed in 1841 when Captain William S. Moorsom (1804-1863) included it in his survey for the Cornwall & Devon Railway which it was proposed to make from Falmouth to Launceston via Truro, St Austell, Lanivet near Bodmin, Blisland and Altarnun. From Launceston the line would go to Lydford, Okehampton, to Creedy near Crediton to join the Bristol & Exeter line two miles on the London side of Exeter. At Lydford a southerly line would diverge to Tavistock and Plymouth. This project failed when the South Devon company secured its Act in 1844, and Tavistock's prospects of an early line receded.

The Formation of the South Devon Railway

The failure of James Rendel's ambitious Dartmoor proposals did not deter the people of Plymouth, and in October 1842 a meeting was held to ascertain the feelings of landowners and inhabitants of the South Hams district respecting a new line through their area. By 2nd September, 1843 the Plymouth Devonport & Exeter Railway had been formed, provisional Directors appointed and an agreement negotiated with the Great Western, the Bristol & Exeter and the Bristol & Gloucester companies, by which these three companies would contribute £400,000 to the capital of the new company and take a leading part in the construction and management of the line.

A prospectus was issued on 13th October, 1843 for a railway from Exeter to Plymouth via the South Hams route as surveyed by Brunel in 1836. The capital was to be £1,100,000, the three associated companies contributing £400,000.

The prospectus stated that the proposed line from Exeter to Plymouth would be 'about 51½ miles long, and in its course the route would combine a large amount of local accommodation with 'less engineering difficulties' than any of the other lines that had been proposed in the surrounding district.

The final decision to construct the line was taken on 21st November, 1843, when it was also decided to change the name of the company to the South Devon Railway Company. The Bill and plans were deposited on 30th November, 1843 and came before the Committee of the House of Commons on 26th April, 1844.

There was little opposition (Devonport Council having withdrawn its opposition shortly before) and the South Devon Railway Bill became law on 4th July, 1844. And so was born the South Devon Railway Company, with the assistance of the Great Western Railway Company in pursuit of its policy of westward expansion - a policy successfully followed later by the South Devon Railway.

It is interesting to note at this stage, that on 19th February, 1844 the provisional Directors of the South Devon had entered into agreement with the Earl of Morley that 'no station which the said company may deem it right to fix at or near the village of Colebrook shall be erected on land belonging to him unless the engineer for the said Company shall certify that such erection will be prejudicial to the interest of the said Company.' This decided the siting of the Plympton station at the foot of Hemerdon bank, and later, was one of the reasons why repeated applications were refused for a station at the junction of the South Devon and Tavistock line with the main line.

Chapter Two

The Tavistock Railway
Ten Years of Frustration

The successful promotion of the South Devon Railway was welcomed in the Tavistock area, and there were renewed hopes that this Devon market town could be connected to the national railway system. James Rendel, meanwhile, had not been idle, and early in 1844 he was again engaged on survey work for a new line, this time from Tavistock to Plymouth.

New Proposals

On 4th May, 1844 - just two months before the incorporation of the South Devon Railway - a prospectus was issued for the hoped-for line from Tavistock to Plymouth. On this occasion, the promoters envisaged a railway that would run:

> . . . from the high ground above Abbey Bridge, passing first above Ash in the parish of Whitchurch, crossing the old Plymouth road and the new road with the valley of the Walkham about midway between the two mile-stone and Bedford Bridge, cutting across the old Wheal Franco mine, passing in front of the Roborough Inn, and crossing Harrowbeer on the Dartmoor road, approaching near to the Plymouth and Dartmoor line, which it leaves a little to the left and continues its course to Crabtree, where it meets the South Devon line, about two miles from Plymouth on the London road.

There was to be further consideration as to whether the proposed Tavistock branch should cross the South Devon main line at Crabtree and have a terminus of its own, or whether branch trains would proceed along the main line to Eldad, where the South Devon terminus had been proposed.

The line would be 15 miles long if it ended at Eldad, but no more than 13 miles if it terminated at Crabtree. The estimated receipts of the line were £260 per week and the expense of working it £100, leaving a balance of £160 which would yield 5½ per cent on the estimated capital of £150,000. Capital would be raised by the issue of shares in the ordinary way, or by a form of joint annuity known as 'Tontine'.

The Duke of Bedford had offered land for the Tavistock terminus and £1,000 for expenses. Other land-owners agreed to afford 'every local facility', with the exception of Lord Morley, who was on the Board of the rival London & South Western Railway.

The Tavistock promoters were determined to lose no time, and they immediately approached the South Devon company for a meeting; as a result of this, a conference was held in Plymouth at which the Tavistock deputation submitted the proposals outlined in their prospectus based upon the principle of a separate undertaking with power to establish routes and by-laws at variance with the main company.

These proposals were not acceptable to the South Devon Directors, who counter-proposed that the Tavistock line should be a branch of the main line, and be worked upon the same principle and under the same regulations as the rest of the SDR system. This proposal being accepted, it was then agreed that the Tavistock company should be allowed a certain number of shares, while the South Devon Railway would find the necessary capital and construct the whole line.

The principle that any line to Tavistock should form, in some way or other, a part of the South Devon line, first announced at the above meeting with the Tavistock company, was embodied in the minutes of the South Devon Board on 24th September, 1844. It became the guide-line of all subsequent negotiations with various parties and was never departed from.

At the first general meeting of the South Devon Railway held on 8th August, 1844, it was announced that Brunel had been engaged during the past week in surveying a portion of the intended branch to Tavistock. At the same meeting a decision was reached which was to have far-reaching consequences upon the South Devon's future, and which led to the rejection of that company's Bill for a line to Tavistock. It was the adoption of a resolution, that 'the atmospheric system of traction be adopted upon the whole of the South Devon Railway.'

On 30th November, 1844 notice was given of intention to apply to Parliament for a Bill for a railway 'commencing by a junction with the line of the South Devon Railway, at or near to Crabtree Marsh in the parish of Eggbuckland and terminating at, in or near to the Borough of Tavistock'.

The suggested line would incorporate gradients rising for seven miles from Plymouth, with 1 in 30 at five miles and 1 in 34 at six miles, and a tunnel between mileposts seven and eight at Yelverton. Apart from this, the route presented no great engineering difficulties, and in an atmosphere of growing enthusiasm the necessary plans were deposited on 30th November; it was at the same time agreed that application would be made for a railway from Tavistock to the town of Launceston - details of which will be given later.

Good financial support was given by the people of Tavistock who had subscribed their share of the capital, £50,000, by 12th February, 1845.

Approval for the Tavistock plan was secured on the same day, but not until strong criticism had been made by Sir Ralph Lopes, one of the principal land-owners, who objected on both public and private grounds. He had supported the first scheme over Dartmoor (Rendel's), as he believed it would lead to great mining development upon comparatively poor land that would benefit both Tavistock and Plymouth, and because it would pass over Roborough Down and thus not interfere more than was necessary with his enclosed lands. Since then another line had been surveyed (Rendel's Tavistock plan of May 1844) which would also pass over Roborough Down.

He was very surprised to find that a third survey had been made through the Plym valley which would pass through his enclosed land. It was also, in his opinion, longer than the two lines previously surveyed and presented greater engineering difficulties. He would, in consequence, oppose it with all the means in his power.

Brunel explained at length his reasons for selecting the Plym valley route; it was the line most beneficial to the public interest, was in accordance with the main principles which applied, and 'afforded the public a good, cheap, easy, in short, the best possible connection, in deciding which, the public and not private, interests must be the first consideration.'

The Launceston project was also strongly criticised by Mr W.A.N. Arundell of Lifton Park, who referred disparagingly to:

> . . . the useless character of the Milton Abbot station, the objectionable site chosen for the Launceston terminus, the deep and expensive nature of cuttings, great length of tunneling in the Kelly area, the exclusion of the districts north of the line, the destruction of the quarry at Mill Hill and the very limited return upon the capital invested.

I.K. Brunel, in dealing with these objections, rapidly demolished them in the same manner as he had previously dealt with the objections to the Tavistock scheme, adding that Mr Arundell had, from the first, been opposed to others, he having been one of the most active supporters of the proposed Central Cornwall line.

In view, however, of later developments in connection with both schemes, the arguments brought forward seem to carry a good deal of weight, and one is made aware of the apparent ease with which logical conclusions put forward by the laymen were dealt with by the professionals.

The draft copies of both Bills were approved at a meeting held on 21st June, 1845, but the Tavistock-Launceston section was later deferred pending a decision on a proposed line from Cornwall to North Devon. The Tavistock portion was included in a South Devon 'omnibus' Bill, the preamble of which was approved by the Commons Committee on 8th July, 1845.

Despite Sir Ralph Lopes' objections made in February, the Bill was unopposed and should have had an easy passage through Parliament. The Directors were very confident of it becoming law, but they were to learn then, and on later occasions, that nothing was more certain than the uncertainty of the passage of Bills through the Legislature.

The Problems Mount

Strong doubts had been voiced at recent meetings of the South Devon as to the efficiency of the atmospheric system - a feeling which grew with the rejection in June 1845 of a Bill for the construction of the Northumberland atmospheric railway. Brunel and the South Devon Directors stood by the atmospheric principle, but it was a different matter with the Parliamentary Committee, for, when the Bill came before them, the attacks made upon it, and the testimony given by some witnesses, led the Committee to the conclusion that the proposed Tavistock line was unsuited to the atmospheric method, and they reserved judgement until the next session.

While it was felt that there would have been no delay had any member of the Committee which investigated the atmospheric system of traction been appointed to the Committee examining the Tavistock Bill, the postponement was not regarded as altogether unfavourable; the company would not suffer any great inconvenience or additional expense as the Bill would be taken up in the next session at the point at which it was left off. The postponement was regretted, mainly for the reason that the Tavistock branch would not now be ready for opening at the same time as the main South Devon line to Plymouth, as had been anticipated and planned.

To ensure the matter being raised in the next session, notice of intent to apply for Powers was given on 4th November. A similar notice was given at the same time in respect of the Launceston & South Devon Bill, which was also to be considered in the coming session of Parliament. Interestingly, it was announced that the Launceston & South Devon Bill would contain a new provision, enabling the Launceston promoters to:

> . . . sell, let or transfer the said intended railway and works or any part thereof, to the South Devon Railway Company, or the North Devon Railway Company, or to any Company which may be authorised to purchase or rent the said South Devon Railway, the North Devon Railway, or the Cornwall Railway Company.

This new provision was considered necessary because a company known as the North Devon Railway had been promoted with the aim of completing a rail link between Cornwall and Devon via Launceston. In view of this development it was deemed prudent that the projected route of the Launceston branch should be deviated, and instead of proceeding to Milton Abbot the branch would form a junction with the North Devon line at Lydford.

The proposed deviation would lengthen the Launceston line by three or four miles, but at the same time the Launceston route would be incorporated into a busy trunk line that would (hopefully) carry traffic from North Cornwall and North Devon. It would also become part of a proposed main line from London to Falmouth with a branch from Liskeard to Launceston, and part of a suggested central trunk line from Bideford to Plymouth.

Rejection By Parliament

The Tavistock proposals, included in a South Devon Bill for expansion and alterations, came before Parliament on 22nd June, 1846. Brunel had to prove there was a slight alteration of the branch of the previous year. The gradients were necessarily of a different character; the severest of them 'he believed' was 1 in 30, but he did not think the company could afford a better line. The branch was 13 miles long and the estimated cost was £200,000. On the following day it was decided that the preamble of the Bill had not been proved.

In the same session the North Devon Bill, to which the South Devon company had extended their support, was also rejected. The reason given was that the engineer appointed by Brunel to survey a portion of the line had been taken suddenly ill and was unable to communicate such information as would enable another to carry on the survey. The result was that plans were imperfect and incomplete, and the Bill was defeated on Standing Orders. The failure of this scheme also meant the loss of the Launceston to Tavistock scheme.

The Directors had, however, succeeded in 'keeping open' the ground, and they instructed Brunel to take a further survey so that they could be ready to adopt any improvements which might be suggested.

The Launceston shareholders were very disappointed at the failure of their proposals, and at their meeting on 20th August, 1846 they strongly criticised Brunel, blaming him for the failure of the Launceston Bill; the South Devon solicitor had to explain that the defeat arose mainly from circumstances over which Brunel had no control, namely, determined opposition, conflicting opinions as to the relative merits of the broad and narrow gauge, and from rival companies.

A fresh application was made to Parliament on 7th November, 1846 for a line from Crabtree to St Johns, otherwise Folly, near Abbey Bridge, Tavistock, proceeding thence to a place near the South Gate in Launceston, and the relevant maps and plans of section were deposited on 30th November, l846.

The shareholders adopted these plans on 9th January, 1847 after being strongly urged to do so by the Directors, it being necessary for the 'ground to be occupied' as the South Western interest had put forward a proposal for a line from Plymouth to Tavistock as part of the Cornwall & Devon & Plymouth Railway.

It is now necessary to trace the activities of the rival promoters. In 1845 a narrow gauge scheme was proposed from Exeter to Falmouth via Crediton, Okehampton, Launceston, Bodmin and Truro to Falmouth. This was condemned in favour of the Cornwall Railway but was revived the following year with the support of the South Western company, and with a branch to Plymouth. The Bill failed on Standing Orders and was thrown out, as was the South Devon & Tavistock and the Launceston extension scheme, which, as will be remembered, had passed the Commons Committee in 1845, but had been postponed by a reserved judgement.

Rival Schemes

The Cornwall & Devon scheme was revived again by the South Western interest, who, on 26th January, 1847 held a supporting meeting in Tavistock. The declared main object was to 'advance the objects of the South Western Company' and the promoters took the unusual (and one could imagine) the welcome step of informing the meeting that the whole of the money had been subscribed and they would not be asked for 'a single stiver'. What they needed was moral support and an encouraging expression of approval to cheer them on their way, as they might 'meet with opposition, even in those quarters where it might be least expected.'

The strong inducement of a direct line to London, thus avoiding the necessity of being taken back to Plymouth in order to get to the Metropolis coupled with the fact that they were not being asked for any financial contribution, produced the anticipated overwhelming support for the narrow gauge interest after Mr C.V. Bridgman, a local solicitor, with no premonition that he would one day support the broad gauge interest, avowed himself as an agent of the South Western company, and 'took pride in being instrumental in the defeat of the South Devon Directors on two previous occasions.'

In February the LSWR Bill met with stiff opposition. The estimate for the line was £4,666,000 - a tremendous sum, and many allegations in this opposed case were sustained. There were disputed errors in the levels, and the Bill was defeated at an early stage.

The Tavistock Bill was dealt with in the same session. By March it was reported that it had been thrown out on 'technical grounds'. This was incorrect. There had been six formidable memorials against the scheme including objections from three principal land-owners; Lord Morley who presented a long memorial against it; the Duke of Bedford who was in favour of a narrow gauge line through central Devon to Cornwall which would have placed Tavistock in a favourable position, and Sir Ralph Lopes, who had spoken against the measure on 15th February, 1845, and who supported the Cornwall & Devon Central & Plymouth application as being preferable from his point of view, but who, at the same time, expressed his determination 'not to do anything inimical to the interest of the South Devon but would render his assent to both schemes.'

Apart from the objections the only thing wrong with the Tavistock Bill was non-compliance on a few insignificant points - namely three clerical errors and the omission of the name of two proprietors and one lessee from the book of reference'. However, the promoters were confident that the Bill would pass the Committee stage.

On 21st June, 1847 Brunel was examined and the talented engineer spoke with the utmost confidence as to the success of the atmospheric system, and, in reply to Counsel, said the only reason why it was not in use was 'that they were not quite ready.'

On the following day there was an unexpected turn of events, the case being brought to a sudden close. The Committee had stopped the evidence of the promoters, stating that they were satisfied that a railway between Tavistock and Plymouth was desirable and of the sufficiency of the traffic. But when the first witnesses for the opposition had been called, the Committee stated they were agreed in the opinion that the branch to Tavistock ought to be postponed.

At the subsequent 'inquest' it was emphasised that the Committee had not rejected the Bill, but had merely postponed it. The evidence in favour had only been partially taken, and no witnesses were called against it; the postponement was wholly extrinsic to the merits of the line. The question would stand over for the present year, when the broad gauge interest would be prepared to submit a further scheme which would also afford improved connection with the north of Devon and with Exeter, a defect which formed the only real objection to the Bill for the present year.

At the meeting on the 28th August, 1847 the Chairman of the South Devon Railway pointedly referred to the campaign of opposition that had been mounted against the Tavistock scheme. They were, he said:

. . . all well aware that they had to a certain extent been successful in their applications to Parliament, and that aggressive measures against them prejudicial to their interests had been frustrated. As to the future, they themselves would not enter upon any aggressive proceedings, but they would not quietly allow their property to be attacked to the prejudice of their interests.

There was little further activity in the matter until August 1849, when two anonymous letters in favour, and one warning against unwise investments in railway projects, appeared in the local Press. These were followed on 6th September, 1849 by a report that the Tavistock railway project was 'again under consideration' and engineers 'had been going over the ground.' Nothing further was heard for some considerable time, but it is clear from what followed that parties were gathering forces for what was to be a tremendous struggle.

In the early part of 1852 the Chairman of the South Devon Railway Company, whose line had opened to Plymouth on 2nd April, 1849, received a letter from Messrs H. & W. Toogood, Parliamentary Agents of London, acting on behalf of interested parties, asking what support the South Devon company would give for a line to Tavistock.

At this stage, the South Devon Directors were not prepared to raise capital for other lines, but realising that a branch to Tavistock would be a valuable adjunct - if worked upon proper principles - they replied that if such a scheme were brought forward they would recommend it to their shareholders for support. The Agents were also advised to get in touch with other interested parties in the Tavistock area, particularly with Mr C.V. Bridgman, the local solicitor who had earlier supported the LSWR.

In the light of previous happenings and of what followed, this was possibly a mistake on the part of the South Devon Railway. C.V. Bridgman had great influence in Tavistock. He had supported the first move for an independent line to the town but felt that he had been badly treated when he was not appointed as one of the solicitors of the original scheme; he then withdrew all support when the South Devon took over the project, and as previously stated, openly championed the interests of the narrow gauge.

The Plymouth & Tavistock Railway

On 25th May, 1852, a prospectus was issued for a company provisionally registered as the Plymouth & Tavistock Railway Company, with capital of £150,000 in twenty pound shares, signed by C.V. Bridgman of Tavistock and C.L. Radcliffe of Plymouth, as solicitors. The latter also represented the interests of Sir Ralph Lopes Bart., a principal landowner whose co-operation and support would be invaluable especially if the proposed route was to be over Roborough Down.

The publication of this prospectus shows evidence of great haste. No details were given of the proposed route, but the new company undertook to examine previous surveys in order to determine which would be of the greatest benefit to the local community. The issue may have been the result of an approach made by Messrs Toogood as suggested by the South Devon company, but more likely it was promoted by a desire to be first in the field. The prospectus was supported by 41 gentlemen from Tavistock and 57 from Plymouth.

One of the promoters of the new company, and later its first Chairman, was Thomas Gill of Tavistock and Plymouth. A member of a well-known Tavistock family of merchant bankers, he was prominent in the public and commercial life of both towns. The founder of the Millbay Soap Works in 1818, he had worked West Hoe, Plymouth, for limestone, built the Millbay Pier and then sold it to the Great Western Docks Company. He also owned an engineering works at Tavistock. He was mayor of Plymouth in 1836, and one of its members of Parliament from 1841 to 1846, when he resigned. The first Chairman of the South Devon Railway Company, he firmly supported Brunel when the atmospheric system of traction, variously described by its critics as 'a farce', 'a caper,' and 'the biggest humbug in the world', ran into difficulties in 1848-49. As the only member of the Board who wished to continue the experiment, he resigned when his published arguments in its favour were demolished, and was afterwards criticised for leaving the Board to cope with the tremendous difficulties which followed.

As Chairman of the South Devon Railway he gave full support to the line proposed from Tavistock in 1844, based upon the principle that any railway to Tavistock should form, in some way or other, a part of the South Devon Railway, but after leaving the Board he became its most formidable opponent. A forceful personality, fierce debater and eloquent speaker, much was to be heard from him during the formative years of the Tavistock line.

Shortly after the Plymouth & Tavistock company had been registered, a request was received was received by the South Devon company from Messrs Gill and Bridgman for a conference. This was readily granted, but as these gentlemen were ill-prepared with no plans, had not decided upon the course of the line and had no engineer or any proposals to make, it was clear that they wished only to ascertain the plans of the South Devon company. They were informed that it was not for the South Devon to make, but to receive proposals which, when made, would receive full consideration along with those of other interested parties.

Intense, almost feverish activity, followed the publication of the prospectus of the Plymouth & Tavistock company on 25th May, 1852. The relative dates being as shown below:

25th May. Plymouth & Tavistock Railway provisionally registered. (First party.)
26th May. Meeting at the Globe, Plymouth, of a second party to consider the project.
29th May. Meeting at Tavistock to introduce the scheme. (First party.)
31st May. Meeting at Plymouth of supporters of the first party.
4th June. Meeting of the second party. Deputation appointed to meet committee of the first party on 9th June.
7th June. Meeting of deputation from second party to consider procedure at meeting to be held on 9th June.
9th June. Meeting referred to above, to consider amalgamation of parties and formation of committees.

The meeting held on 9th June was presided over by Thomas Gill who, before the time appointed for the deputation from the second party to attend, reminded his supporters that there should be no scheme if they had any opposition, and that they must be independent of the South Devon, its Engineer and its Solicitors. After the deputation arrived there were long discussions, but the meeting failed in its main purpose of unity and joint action, and it was decided to allow the Plymouth & Tavistock Railway to go its own way.

The South Devon company was now in no doubt as to who was its chief opponent and had not long to wait, for on 10th July, 1852, a letter from 'A Plymouthian', appeared in the *Plymouth, Devonport and Stonehouse Herald*, alleging that a rumour was in circulation that the Solicitors of the South Devon company were doing all in their power to defeat, once again, the projected line of railway from Plymouth to Tavistock. They were said to have secured the support of a nobleman and had undertaken, 'of course at the expense of the company' to construct a branch line to the clay works (which it was presumed would cost £10,000), the Solicitors being confident they would be able to convince their shareholders that such a branch will tend to enhance the value of their line.

This letter was dated 5th July, 1852, the very date on which an agreement was signed in London by Lord Morley on behalf of himself, the Lee Moor Porcelain Clay Company, William Phillips and Thomas Woollcombe, the Chairman of the South Devon company. It led to acrimonious correspondence between the Solicitors of the South Devon company and Thomas Gill, who, on being challenged, admitted writing the letter. Mr Gill had undoubtedly got hold of information respecting the intentions of the South Devon, and had made use of it to serve his own ends and those of the Plymouth & Tavistock company.

The South Devon & Tavistock Railway

On 17th July, 1852 the prospectus of the South Devon & Tavistock Railway Company, dated 5th July, 1852, was published in the contemporary press, for a broad gauge line from Plymouth to Tavistock, with a branch to Lee Moor for the porcelain works, under a proposed arrangement with the South Devon Railway. The Chairman of the new company, the Earl of Morley (the owner of the clay works) was accompanied on the Board by Thomas Woollcombe and Colonel H.B. Harris, both of whom were Directors of the South Devon company. The Solicitors were Messrs H. & W. Toogood who had originated the scheme, and Whiteford, Bennett & Tucker, Solicitors to the South Devon. The Engineer was A.H. Bampton.

The capital was to be £160,000 in shares of £25 each, and the line, a modification of Brunel's survey of 1846, would diverge from the South Devon line at Longbridge, traverse the Plym valley, and reach Tavistock in a course not exceeding 13 miles. A short line from Lee Moor Clay Works to join the new line would be at once constructed. Arrangements would also be made, if found desirable, to form another branch line to the Government establishments at Princetown.

At a meeting held on 13th July, 1852, the shareholders of the South Devon company accepted a recommendation to take a lease of the intended line and branch in perpetuity. It was pointed out that Lord Morley had not taken advantage of his position in regard to the proposed company, and the large share issue which he would possess, to make better terms for himself. The construction of the Lee Moor branch would rest upon his shoulders up to a certain point. If the company were incorporated and an Act was obtained there would be a price for the Lee Moor branch.

At this time Lord Morley was a member of the Board of the London & South Western company, and to put himself right in this matter he wrote to the Chairman of the South Western Railway company on 13th July, 1852. His letter contained the following passage:

> That as the circumstances under which he had joined the South Western Board had so entirely changed (his object being only to promote the formation of a branch line to Plymouth) and as a rivalry of interests had now sprung up between Southampton and Plymouth, he felt it his duty to disconnect himself from the South Western Company and to align himself with those who were seeking to advance the interest of the trade and the capabilities of the port of Plymouth.

Both parties were still desperately anxious to avoid the waste of time and money which would be incurred by opposition, and each hoped that the other side would give in.

On 20th August, 1852, a letter was sent by the South Devon & Tavistock company to the Plymouth & Tavistock company to see if there could not be a union of interests which would lead to an agreement. This led to a lengthy correspondence during August and September. The South Devon view was that it was almost impossible that the Tavistock branch, as it was proposed to be constructed with trains and engines running over the South Devon line, could be worked with any approach to economy or efficiency otherwise than by the South Devon Railway.

In reply the Plymouth & Tavistock promoters laid down the specific principles upon which they desired to unite with the South Devon Railway. They were:

1. The integrity of their scheme, involving complete freedom of action.
2. Provided a line proceeded through the Plym valley, a station would be formed at Crabtree.
3. All passengers arriving at Crabtree, whether going north, south, east or west, and all passengers on the South Devon line going forward would be conveyed from the same station.
4. The line should consist of the best gradients and curves of which the country through which it passed admitted.

These principles were wholly unacceptable to the South Devon Directors, who however still hoped that a contest might be avoided; if not, their part would be that of declared hostility.

On 18th September, 1852 there was a new development. A meeting was held on that day at Okehampton to take steps for a railway from Tavistock to Copplestone Cross via Okehampton. A deputation from the Plymouth & Tavistock company was invited to attend, the object being to consider the extension of the latter company's line from Tavistock towards Copplestone Cross, thus forming a communication between Plymouth, Exeter and North Devon. After a long discussion Thomas Gill, leader of the Plymouth and Tavistock deputation, spoke in favour of the scheme.

At a meeting of the Plymouth & Tavistock Railway held on 29th October, 1852 the long awaited Engineer's report was presented.

The proposed line from Plymouth to Tavistock would commence near Eldad (which would give easy communication to Stonehouse Pool or Millbay Docks), proceed to Honicknowle, Jump, cross Roborough Down to the Meavy valley and then continue northwards to Tavistock, embracing the best features of Locke's and Brunel's surveys. Access to Sutton Pool, Plymouth, would be by means of a tunnel through Lipson Hill to Coxside. Mr Gill explained that their line would be a mile and a half shorter than the Plym valley line, which would also have involved going onto the South Devon line to reach Plymouth or running neck and neck with it. Their proposal would make them entirely independent of the South Devon Railway.

He then went on to say that as a result of the publication of the South Devon & Tavistock prospectus on 5th July, 1852, the Plymouth & Tavistock Company were unable to allot shares until 30th July - by which time the natural effect of a rival scheme was to create a doubt in the minds of the allottees as to the ultimate success of their undertaking. He then referred to the scheme for the proposed extension of their line from Tavistock to Okehampton, North Tawton and Coleford, where there would be a connection with Exeter and the north of Devon, bringing Tavistock 30 miles nearer Exeter.

He pointed out that they would hardly be able to carry their own line to Tavistock in the face of South Devon opposition, but if their scheme embraced a line of 45 miles instead of one of 15 miles, the probability of success was greatly increased. He was so optimistic and naive as to suggest that when the South Devon & Tavistock saw how much support the public would give to the Plymouth & Tavistock extended scheme 'they would withdraw their opposition.'

The Plymouth, Tavistock, Okehampton & Exeter Railway

The merger of the Plymouth & Tavistock and the Okehampton schemes was agreed by the two groups of promoters, and the prospectus of the combined scheme was approved. It was published on 5th November, 1852, under the cumbersome title 'The Plymouth, Tavistock, Okehampton & Exeter Railway'.

The enlarged company had a capital of £500,000 in twenty pound shares, and its Chairman was Thomas Gill. The Engineer was T.C. Bell, while the solicitors and secretaries (*pro tempore*) were C.V. Bridgman and C.L. Radcliffe. The distances given were: Plymouth to Exeter 53 miles, and Plymouth to Barnstaple 69 miles.

Sadly, matters did not go well for the newly-formed company.

Arrangements for the extended line were not completed until the end of October. Surveys began the first week in November, but bad weather prevented their being completed with accuracy.

The delays caused dissatisfaction among the Plymouth shareholders who called a meeting for 14th January, 1853, when only 14 were present. These did not include Messrs Gill and Radcliffe who, however, attended when a message was sent to them. Gill immediately objected to the irregular manner of calling the meeting but agreed to listen to the complaint. This was that the subscription list had been signed under the impression that the line would be carried through to Exeter via Okehampton, but there was a strong rumour that the proposed extension from Tavistock had been given up. Gill denied this but admitted they were not then in a position to carry out the perfect scheme.

He alleged a wrong report had been circulated to make their members dissatisfied. Evasive answers were given as to why original Directors in Plymouth had retired from the company, and the reason for the withdrawal of much support. He affirmed that the company was in a position to fight the opposing scheme, and they intended to do so, a deposit of £15,000 having been paid the previous day for this purpose.

When a member commenced a review of the affairs of the company since its formation, Gill said it 'was a waste of time listening to such nonsensical rubbish' and left the meeting, which then dissolved.

Ten days later a regularly convened meeting of the company was held in a much better atmosphere. After long explanations as to why the necessary capital could not be raised - attributed mainly to rumours prejudicial and unfounded that had been spread by other parties - they found it necessary to limit the application to Parliament during the present session for a line from Plymouth to Tavistock only, intending, if successful, to apply for the remaining portion to Coleford in the following year. These explanations being accepted, it was then resolved:

That the Bill of the South Devon & Tavistock Railway Company be opposed in Parliament; that the address to the public be read, approved, printed and circulated, and that subscription lists be opened in the main towns concerned.

The arrangements were that the South Devon Bill would be examined on Standing Orders on 27th January, 1853 and their own Bill on 2nd February. If both Bills passed, both would go before the Committee on merits, 'and then the great struggle would begin'.

In February 1853 the Bill for the new line from Longbridge to Tavistock, with power to the South Devon Company to subscribe, was received in Parliament on Standing Orders, but the Plymouth & Tavistock company's Bill was rejected.

Strong support was given to the South Devon & Tavistock cause on 14th March, 1853 when the Duke of Bedford, who had previously been consistent in his preference for a line from Plymouth to Exeter via Okehampton, wrote to Lord Morley from his London address. His letter contained the following passage:

As I think it is of considerable importance that Tavistock should not be left any longer without railway communication, I shall be glad to learn that it will also be incorporated by Parliament in the present session. You are at liberty to make this public if you think it desirable to do so.

A Further Rejection

The South Devon & Tavistock Bill went into Committee on 12th June, 1853. It was severely tested at a seven day trial when the evidence of the promoters was heard. The opposition party put up a strong case but the Committee declared the preamble proved.

At this time a great fight was going on in Parliament respecting the Bill for the Devon & Dorset line put forward by the Great Western and Bristol & Exeter companies. This was a line of little merit; it was mainly through South Western territory and had obviously been introduced to keep out the narrow gauge interest. It had the effect, however, of arousing the South Western to opposition, and the issue became a test between the broad and narrow gauge factions. To support their case the South Western called the Rt. Hon. Sydney Herbert, Secretary of War and Member for South Wilts; Lord Malmesbury, a former Foreign Secretary; General Lord Hardinge the Commander-in-Chief and Sir James Graham the First Lord of the Admiralty, who all testified to the great difficulties experienced when troops, cavalry and equipment travelling by rail were considerably delayed by being forced to change from broad to narrow gauge and vice versa.

It had become a matter of national importance - concerning the defence of the Realm - that there should be railway communications with an unbroken gauge between the Metropolis and the main ports and arsenals in the land. The South Western pledged that if the Devon & Dorset Bill were rejected, they would extend their narrow gauge system from Dorchester to Exeter with a possible extension to Plymouth at a later date. (At this stage the total mileage of mixed gauge on the Great Western Railway was 69 miles, 35 chains compared with 250 miles, 71 chains of broad gauge, and even much later the Great Western was reluctant to introduce more mixed gauge.)

This evidence from such a powerful quarter not only settled the fate of the Devon & Dorset line, but influenced the Committee against the South Devon Bill which, however, despite such powerful opposition, received its third reading in July.

Opposition to the Bill was also being whipped up in the West Country. A meeting at Exeter on 14th July, 1853 was strongly in favour of the narrow gauge line from Coleford to Okehampton, Tavistock and Plymouth, the conversion of the Exeter & Crediton line to the narrow gauge and a connection at Exeter with a proposed line from Dorchester, there being great emphasis on the need for railway communication of unbroken gauge.

On 7th July the Bill had its first reading in the Lords: the decision of the House on the Devon & Dorset Bill, the opposition of land-owners, together with the doubts of the Government on the relative merits of the broad and narrow gauges, proved to be too much and it was thrown out.

This was a sad blow. Speaking on 23rd August, 1853 on the failure of the Bill, the Chairman of the South Devon company said the cause was not on merit; the case was satisfactorily proved before both Houses of Parliament, but a concatenation of events, not likely to recur, then brought against them was too strong for them to successfully contend against.

Thomas Gill seized upon this opportunity to criticise the South Devon Directors, not only for losing their own line to Tavistock, but in making it easier for the narrow gauge to be brought to Plymouth.

'This,' he declared, 'would be one of the greatest blessings which could be conferred on the town, which at present was retrograde,' due entirely he believed, to the South Devon's policy which failed to grapple with the traffic brought to it. 'Delays and shortage of transport were frequent and the traffic problem was intolerable.'

He then blamed the Directors for failing to afford parties facilities to promote a great public improvement such as the Tavistock Railway, of failing to negotiate with him on his own proposals and on their policy since he had ceased to be Chairman of the South Devon, and ended by saying 'The names of the South Devon Directors will be remembered - pause - so long as time endured - long pause and laughter - as the great enemies of Plymouth, unless they were disposed to adopt a different policy from that which they had lately pursued'.

The SDR Chairman replied by reminding Mr Gill of the course adopted by him when he was Chairman of the South Devon company at the time of the atmospheric difficulties, of the speeches he then made against the narrow gauge, so totally at variance to what he now professed to believe.

Today, with the benefit of hindsight and the experience of over a hundred years of history, it is difficult to say who was right or who was wrong. The narrow gauge came to Plymouth in 1876, ironically over the South Devon line between Lydford and Marsh Mills, when mixed gauge was introduced for London & South Western trains. Thomas Gill did not see the fulfilment of his prophecy; he died in 1861.

The pledge of the South Western company to introduce a Bill in the 1854 session for the extension of their line to Exeter not only defeated the Devon & Dorset and the South Devon & Tavistock Bills, it also put an end to the Plymouth, Tavistock, Okehampton & Exeter scheme, and this project was not proceeded with in the 1854 Session. The South Western later repudiated their pledge, which did not please the Board of Trade - but that is another story.

Success at Last

In making arrangements for the renewal of their application to Parliament the Directors of the South Devon & Tavistock company found it expedient to secure the professional services of Mr C.V. Bridgman as an additional solicitor. As already recorded, this gentleman had previously strongly opposed all efforts of the South Devon to secure a Tavistock line, and had openly allied himself with

ANNO DECIMO SEPTIMO & DECIMO OCTAVO

VICTORIÆ REGINÆ.

✹✹

Cap. clxxxix.

An Act for making a Railway from the *South Devon* Railway near *Plymouth* to *Tavistock*, with a Branch, to be called " The *South Devon and Tavistock* Railway," and for other Purposes.

[24th *July* 1854.]

WHEREAS the making of a Railway from the *South Devon* Railway near *Long Bridge* near *Plymouth* in the County of *Devon* to *Tavistock* in that County, with a Branch therefrom as herein-after described, would be of great public Advantage: And whereas the Persons herein-after named, with others, are willing at their own Expense to carry such Undertaking into execution: And whereas the following Acts have been passed relating to the *South Devon* Railway Company, in this Act called " The *South Devon* Company"; (to wit,) the several Acts of the Seventh and Eighth of *Victoria*, Chapter Sixty-eight; of the Ninth and Tenth of *Victoria*, Chapter Four hundred and two; of the Tenth and Eleventh of *Victoria*, Chapter Two hundred and forty-two; and of the Fourteenth and Fifteenth of *Victoria*, Chapter Fifty-three: And whereas the making of the Railway and Branch would be beneficial to the *South Devon* Company, and it is expedient that that Company be authorized to become Shareholders in the Undertaking to the Extent and

[*Local.*]   36 *E*   upon

The title page of the South Devon & Tavistock Railway Act, 1854. *Chris Turner Collection* the narrow gauge interest and acted as a joint solicitor of the Plymouth, Tavistock, Okehampton & Exeter company.

To make this diplomatic change the South Devon company dispensed with the services of two local solicitors at Tavistock, who were summarily dismissed and who, in their strongly-worded reply, issued the following thinly-veiled threat of legal action against the South Devon & Tavistock Railway:

> . . . if the replacement of solicitors who had rendered faithful service by one who had been active in opposition, indicated the principle upon which the affairs were to be conducted in future, they had no regret in severing their connection with the company but reserved the right to take action if circumstances should prove injurious to them.

The notice of intention to apply to Parliament in the 1854 session for leave to bring in a Bill for the line from Longbridge, with a branch to Lee Moor clay works, was issued on 3rd November, 1853; plans were deposited on 30th November.   Practical and moral support was again given by the Duke of Bedford, who made a grant of land for the line and station at Tavistock and a donation of £500 for Parliamentary expenses.

The South Devon & Tavistock Railway Bill was again brought forward in 1854 and was read for a second time. By 18th May it had passed the Committee stage 'unaltered as regards its opponents', and was therefore considered to be safe.

The opposition party, under Gill, had another go and made an attempt to frustrate the Bill by forming the Plymouth, Tavistock & Devon Central Railway, but this failed. There was a period of anxiety in May, when it was rumoured that the House of Lords would compel the company to introduce a clause for the narrow gauge to be adopted over the whole of the line, and even to carry it into Plymouth.

The Lords did not, in fact, insist on the narrow gauge being laid throughout, but at the last moment, when the Bill came before Lord Redesdale, he, without receiving any evidence upon the subject, and 'by the immense authority he possessed in such matters', forced into the Bill a clause, that should a narrow gauge line ever connect itself with the Tavistock branch the company would be obliged to admit the narrow gauge upon their system.   The South Devon Directors did not like this and they considered opposing it, but having already spent so much money and time in reaching this stage, wisely decided not to do so. The Bill received the Royal Assent on 24th July, 1854.

The resulting Act (17 & 18 Vic. cap.189) provided consent for a railway, and a 'branch railway or tramway' which, for convenience, were designated Railway No. 1 and Railway No. 2.

Railway No. 1 was defined as:

> A Railway commencing by a junction with the Main Line of the South Devon Railway in a Close called the Long Bridge Great Marsh, belonging to the Right Honourable the Earl of Morley, in the occupation of James Martin, and situate in the Parish of Plympton Saint Mary in the County of Devon near the bridge called Long Bridge in that Parish, and terminating in a Close, formerly an orchard, in the occupation of Henry Browne, Thomas Pengelly and John Crossman, situate in the Parish of Tavistock in that County,

at or near a place called Saint John's, on the western side of the old turnpike road leading from Plymouth to Tavistock.

Railway No. 2, which would form the proposed branch to Lee Moor clay works, was described as:

A branch railway or tramway commencing and diverging from and out of the intended Railway in or near a Close called the Plym Bridge Great Marsh, in the occupation of James Butland, situate in the Parish of Plympton Saint Mary near Plym Bridge, on the south side of the road leading from Plym Bridge to Colebrook, and terminating at or near a place called Black Alder Torr, situate in the Parish of Shaugh otherwise Shaugh Prior in that County, near to the Works of the Lee Moor Porcelain Clay Company.

The new railway would be 'constructed, maintained and worked upon the broad gauge' of 7 ft 0¼ in., with the proviso that if at any time it should be required for the public service an 'additional rail or rails for the passage of engines or carriages adapted to the narrow gauge' would be laid down on all or any part of the line.

A period of five years was allowed for completion of the works, and Sir Antony Buller, Harry Bulteel Harris, Thomas Woollcombe, William Prance, George Frean, James Dabb, David Derry, Thomas Hillersden Bulteel and William Rendle were mentioned by name as the first Directors of the South Devon & Tavistock Railway Company.

The authorised capital was fixed at £160,000 in twenty five pound shares, together with a further £53,300 by loan or mortgage.

Chapter Three

Construction, Opening and Early Years of the Tavistock Railway

The authorised route of the South Devon & Tavistock Railway ran more or less due north from its junction with the South Devon main line. Following the valleys of the River Plym and Meavy, the route continued for 13 miles, via Bickleigh and Horrabridge, to Tavistock. Civil engineering works would be relatively heavy, with tunnels at Shaugh, Yelverton and Grenofen, and a number of large bridges and viaducts including a major viaduct across the Walkham Valley between Yelverton and Tavistock.

Preliminaries to Construction

The period immediately following the incorporation of the company was one of financial and commercial depression. There was difficulty in obtaining the required capital, and it had been almost impossible to make any progress in the construction of the line apart from the Lee Moor branch, which had been built under a separate contract, to a gauge different from the main line. This was so badly constructed that the South Devon company refused to work it, as did Mr Bampton, the South Devon & Tavistock Engineer, when approached by Mr Phillips - a party to the agreement for building the tramway - who took forcible possession of the line in March 1855.

A new agreement entered into with Lord Morley on 5th June, 1856 enabled the company to give up the line from near Plym Bridge to the Lee Moor clay works site, an opportunity they were glad to seize as the tramway had become an embarrassing liability.*

At the time of incorporation the amount of capital subscribed amounted to £116,000, about three-quarters of the amount needed and sufficient only for the Bill. The Act stipulated that the compulsory purchase of land had to be completed by 24th July, 1857, and the construction of the line by July 1859. It was therefore necessary for the capital to be made up immediately, otherwise the company would be unable to proceed with the purchase of the land, the undertaking would have to be relinquished and the company wound up. The main work could not be started until more capital was available, but in order to save time negotiations were entered into with the contractors, and surveys of the work taken in hand, but these were not completed until August 1855.

By then the capital had been increased by £16,000, which included a liberal subscription of £11,000 from the Duke of Bedford. A public appeal was then made, with poor response from Plymouth, but with success from Tavistock people, who subscribed an additional £6,000 leaving £20,000 to be raised.

The matter was put to the assembled shareholders at the first half-yearly meeting of the company held on 5th February, 1856, when it was explained that if they contributed another £7,000 the Directors could see their way to raise £3,000 and the Duke of Bedford would then subscribe a further £10,000. Strong

* For the full story, see R.M.S. Hall's book *The Lee Moor Tramway* (Oakwood Press).

support was promised, and the requisite sum was raised by August 1856.

Construction Begins

As a result work was able to commence, and steps were taken on 25th August, 1856 when the first sod was lifted on Mrs Davey's farm on Roborough Down. In view of financial stringency the Directors decided that there should be no public ceremony on this occasion, but preferred to wait until the work was completed before having any celebration.

The actual work on the line commenced on 24th September, 1856, and good progress was made during the following six months. By this time much land had been purchased and the principle landowners, including the Commoners of Roborough Down, had greatly facilitated matters - Sir Massey Lopes making a free gift of his rights on the Downs.

At the August meeting in 1857 it was reported that their Engineer, A.H. Bampton, who had largely been responsible for bringing forward the 1852 scheme, had died. As successor the company were fortunate in securing the services of I.K. Brunel.

The Acting Engineer reported that during the past year the works had been extended; both the longer tunnels were in progress; the shafts had been sunk, the headings driven, portions of the tunnels enlarged to full size and the masonry completed. The plans of several stations had been settled and the permanent way would soon be ready for the rails.

In spite of this favourable report there was criticism of the work at Tavistock, which was proceeding very slowly, this being attributed to lack of supervision by Brunel, the contractor being unable to receive proper instructions in consequence. At that time Brunel was fully occupied in preparing to float into position the truss for the western span of the Saltash Bridge, and it was unlikely that Tavistock would receive his personal attention until that great engineering feat was accomplished, but it was considered that the two assistant engineers, Mr Grose and William Glennie, were quite capable of dealing with the work. In addition, R.P. Brereton, Chief Assistant to Brunel, had undertaken the general supervision of the work.

It will be remembered that the prospectus of the company provided 'that the line would be so arranged, that, if found desirable, another branch railway may be formed to the Government establishments at Princetown, or an existing railway modified for this purpose.'

This question was raised at the half-yearly meeting held on 29th August, 1857, the suggestion being that there should be a line to Princetown from Yelverton. After a long discussion it was agreed that the meeting could do little in the matter at that stage apart from recommending the Directors to consider the matter (the Princetown Railway was not opened until 11th August ,1883).

At the same meeting it was agreed that the Heads of an Agreement for leasing the line in perpetuity to the South Devon company, agreed to in August 1856, would be embodied in a Bill to be presented in the next Session of Parliament. This Bill was unopposed and became law on 12th July, 1858.

On 8th February, 1858, Brunel made his first report as Engineer to the South Devon & Tavistock Railway. It read as follows:

Considerable progress has been made during the past six months. About 2¼ miles of the southern end of the line were ready for the permanent way.

At Yelverton tunnel the headings had been driven through and one-third of the tunnel completed. At Shaugh and Grenofen the shafts had been sunk and the headings and enlargements were in progress. Masonry on all piers of the viaducts but one was complete or in progress and at some, the timber framing had been erected. Masonry on most of the bridges and culverts had been completed.

Rails were being manufactured and deliveries were expected shortly. Timber and other material was on the ground. Station buildings were in progress and should be completed by the end of the summer.

When the line was first proposed, it was decided for the sake of economy to build it on the plan adopted by the West Cornwall company, with the Barlow system of permanent way. The Barlow system incorporated Barlow rails, which were large 'V'-shaped bridge rails. Designed to avoid the need for wooden sleepers, these rails were supposed to maintain the gauge by digging their widely splayed 'feet' into the ballast. In practice, this ingenious system was a total failure because the rails tended to spread themselves laterally beneath the weight of passing trains.

The West Cornwall Railway had experienced considerable difficulty with this method, and there had been several derailments involving locomotives. Brunel had made an inspection and found that the cause of failure was the use of inferior iron for the rails and the wrong method of ballasting, which caused spreading of the line. It was decided that the Tavistock line must be made as secure as possible for the heavy traffic expected, and the additional estimated expenditure was approved.

By 25th August, 1858 it was stated by Brunel that the junction with the South Devon line had been made and about three miles of rail laid. The tunnels at Shaugh and Grenofen had caused some difficulty, where the ground was not turning out so favourably for rapid progress, but steps were being taken to improve matters. Other works were well in hand.

The question of a junction station with the South Devon line continued to be raised at company meetings - the inconvenience, loss of time and money through having to travel from the junction to Plymouth and back, some eight miles, which would be incurred by passengers from Tavistock travelling eastwards, being strongly emphasised. The Chairman of the South Devon, who was present, said that his company would not agree to the erection of any additional stations, but if the Tavistock company would like to erect a station at Marsh Mills (not, let it be noted, on the main line) at their own cost, the South Devon would be ready to consider the matter. (Note: Article 2 of the agreement between Lord Morley and the South Devon & Tavistock company, dated 5th July, 1852, provided 'that no station was to be built between the Turnpike and the South Devon line without Lord Morley's permission'.)

In anticipation of the early completion of the Tavistock line the South Devon company, who were to work the route, were making preparations to deal with the additional traffic, and had set aside £7,000 of new capital for additional rolling stock and locomotive power.

Unfavourable weather during the winter caused some delays in the final stages of construction but by 23rd February, 1859 the Engineer reported that there was every hope of the line being completed within two months and ready for opening shortly after. Early in June Brunel passed over the line to make a personal inspection, and expressed himself well satisfied with the manner in which the works had been carried out.

Opening of the Line to Tavistock

Having passed its Board of Trade inspection the Plymouth to Tavistock line was officially opened on 21st June, 1859.

The first train started from Plymouth at 9 o'clock and conveyed those who could not be accommodated in the special train which left at 2 o'clock and consisted of 10 carriages containing the Directors and officials of the company, with about 300 guests. In the first train there were the bands of the 96th Regiment and the Warwickshire Militia, who with the Tavistock Brass Band and the Tavistock Fife and Drum Band, were to take part in a huge procession. The trains ran non-stop to Tavistock, and passed *en route* hundreds of spectators who had assembled at convenient places to witness the inauguration of the railway.

The official train was met upon arrival at Tavistock by the Portreeve of the Court Leet and Court Baron of Tavistock, who read an address offering congratulations on the successful completion of the railway, which it was calculated would bring great benefit to the town. The vice-chairman of the company replied in similar vein, and the official party then took part in the celebratory procession through the streets of Tavistock.

The great procession (which had already been marshalled) must have been one of the largest as well as the best ever seen on such an occasion. Practically all trades in the town were represented. Among them and leading the exhibits were the printers of the *Tavistock Gazette* mounted on a wagon, printing the railway timetable which was distributed gratuitously.

Then came the captains and clerks of mines who rode in four-wheel traps; miners from Wheal Crelake with the tools of their trade; the Bedford Foundry establishment with a banner; proprietors in a carriage, clerks and foremen on horseback, smiths with the emblems of their trade, chainmakers, a wagon with two steam engines, a portable steam engine, patternmakers on horse-back; bakers working with an oven; employees of Bedford Yard with models of the Duke of Bedford cottages; dairymen with models of a pork butcher's shop and a farmyard; coachbuilders riding on stage-coaches and woolcombers.

An unusual feature was the presence of two of Tavistock's oldest inhabitants, John Eddy aged 99 years and Mary Doidge aged 97 years, who rode in the Portreeve's carriage. Some very fine horses which had been employed in the construction work of the line were also in the long procession, which took some considerable time to pass through the main streets decorated with flags, flowers

Tavistock station at the opening of the Tavistock & South Devon Railway, 21st June, 1859.
Illustrated London News

and triumphal arches, before coming to a stop in Bedford Square. Here the procession broke up and the official party adjourned to the nearby Bedford Hotel where a dinner was provided for 120.

The usual toasts were given and suitably responded to. The Portreeve, in proposing the toast to the Directors, thanked them for the number of trains they had agreed to run on weekdays but hoped they would not have many trains on Sundays! (This was received with cries of '*oh, oh!*' and '*plenty of them!*') The Portreeve seemed to be a little sensitive on this point, and soon resumed his seat! The railway was opened for public traffic on the following day, 22nd June, 1859.

Some Details of the Line

The newly-opened branch was a single track, broad gauge route with intermediate stations at Bickleigh and Horrabridge. Its principal engineering features included the tunnels at Shaugh (308 yds), Yelverton (641 yds) and Grenofen (374 yds), together with five timber viaducts of varying lengths. The most impressive engineering feature *en route* to Tavistock was the soaring Walkham Viaduct, which towered 132 ft above local ground level and consisted of 15 timber spans (*see Chapter Seven for further details*).

The line was, in many ways, a typical 'Brunelian' route, with many of the features found on other 7 ft gauge lines in the West of England. Its timber

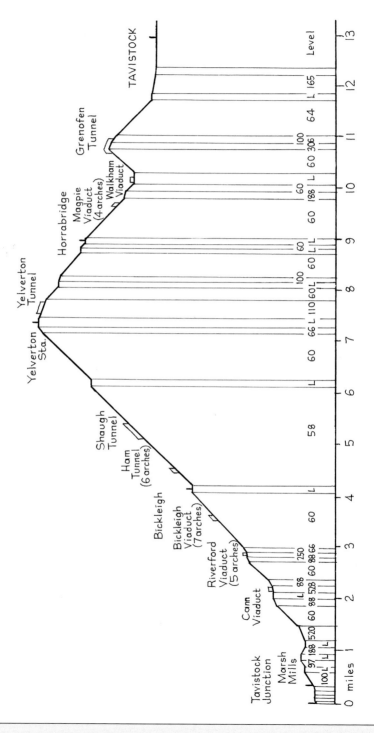

Marsh Mills to Tavistock
Gradient Profile

viaducts, for example, were of classic Brunelian design, while the intermediate stations sported small, Italianate buildings that closely resembled their counterparts on the Cornwall Railway and on other parts of the broad gauge system.

At Tavistock the branch terminated in a characteristic 'Brunel-style' overall roof station - though it is perhaps worth pointing out that the stations at Bickleigh, Horrabridge and Tavistock had probably been designed by Brunel's assistant R.P. Brereton rather than Brunel himself. On the other hand, Brereton undoubtedly followed Brunelian traditions, and to that extent it would be true to say that the South Devon & Tavistock Railway was a classic Brunelian line, built in the style that we have come to associate with the Great Western Railway and its subsidiaries in Wales and the West of England.

Early Years of the Tavistock Line

The traffic on the line immediately following the opening was very heavy. Thousands travelled from Plymouth to Bickleigh, Horrabridge and Tavistock, whence they dispersed over a wide area to visit the many places of interest on the Moor which had hitherto been accessible to relatively few people. In addition, organised parties, which later became very popular, started on 30th June, 1859, when 2,450 members of the Oddfellows Society travelled by special trains to Tavistock to attend a fete in the town.

It is interesting to note that the first train service provided five trains in each direction on weekdays and four on Sundays, but the latter service was reduced to two shortly after.

At the company's half-yearly meeting on 31st August, 1859, the Chairman congratulated the shareholders on the highly favourable circumstances which led to the opening of the line. In a review of the situation he reminded them of the 'difficult times through which the company had passed'. There had been intense opposition and a most severe Parliamentary test, which caused at least a year's delay and had added several thousand pounds to the expenditure.

Immediately after the passing of the Bill a serious trade depression brought a financial crisis which made it difficult to raise the balance of capital required. At one stage it was doubtful if the company would have been able to carry on but for the energy and zeal of the Board, the support given to them by the shareholders and, above all, the financial support given at various stages by the Duke of Bedford.

A shareholder drew attention to a great inconvenience which had been foreseen and spoken of, through lack of a station at the junction with the main line, particularly to the people in the Plympton area who had to spend so much time in travelling the relatively short distance to Tavistock by having to go to Plymouth for connecting services.

The question of the junction station was taken a step further early in October 1859 at a meeting held in the Guildhall, Plympton St Maurice, when examples were given of the length of time taken to travel between Plympton and Tavistock. Travelling by the 9.17 am train from Plympton, due at Plymouth at

9.35 am, passengers had to wait until 11.00 am. for the connecting train which reached Tavistock at 11.50 am. Long delays also occurred in the reverse direction. A resolution, to be sent as a petition to the railway company, read:

> That to the inhabitants of Plympton, Ridgeway and neighbourhood, the want of a station on the Tavistock branch, at or near the junction with the South Devon line, is felt to be a serious handicap and inconvenience, prejudicial to the markets and cattle fairs of Tavistock and Plympton and most prohibitory to the use of the line between these towns, either for business or pleasure.

As a result of this petition and of previous representations from local people, the matter was reconsidered, and a station for passengers was opened at Marsh Mills on 15th March, 1861, but not at the point of junction with the main line. This new facility, while meeting the local needs of Plympton, did not satisfy those travelling to the north and east who still had to put up with the inconvenience of having to go into Plymouth for their connecting trains.

The question continued to be raised at almost every half-yearly meeting of the company, as a good deal of traffic between Tavistock and Exeter, and London, was lost in the early years of the railway. At first passengers found it more convenient to take the stage-coach from Tavistock to Exeter, and later the coach which ran in conjunction with the South Western Railway when that company's line reached Okehampton on 3rd October, 1871, and three years later to Lydford when the narrow gauge line reached that station.

A last approach was made to the South Devon Railway in 1862 in connection with the proposed Launceston line, but the uncompromising answer was 'certainly not' - even though it was then stated that land at Crabtree, near Marsh Mills, was available and that there would not be much objection from Lord Morley. The decision had great influence on the pattern of rail travel from Tavistock, and even as late as the 1930s passengers for the North and the Midlands preferred to travel by South Western line to Exeter, there to connect with the Great Western express trains.

On 27th February, 1860, R.P. Brereton, who had taken over from Brunel after the latter's untimely death in 1859 reported that during the first six months of the line's existence the passenger traffic had been satisfactorily worked by the South Devon company and the line had been opened for goods traffic. Sidings for the accommodation of goods had been laid in at Tavistock and Horrabridge stations and other works left unfinished at the opening of the line had been completed.

The works generally, and the permanent way, had stood the traffic well through the winter; the viaducts were in a satisfactory condition and the heavy embankments had been little affected by the unfavourable weather and the traffic.

The facilities at Horrabridge for dealing with copper ore traffic were reported as being insufficient. Over 200 tons of ore had passed through the station in February, and 300 tons were expected to pass in March. Better access to the station and improved loading facilities were required.

About this time a siding was put in at Crelake at 12 miles 43 chains to deal with copper ore from Wheal Crelake mine, which, although conveniently situated for the Tavistock Canal, preferred to load at the siding and take advantage of special cheap rates offered by the railway company for transit to Plymouth.

An application for siding accommodation at Yelverton for lime and coal traffic was received and referred to the South Devon company. This was eventually provided.

During 1860-1 the goods traffic continued to increase, but the facilities for handling failed to increase with it. There was need for still better accommodation on the whole of the line, and also at Plymouth Docks in connection with the loading from ship to truck. There were heavy delays in transit to goods traffic, especially to that forwarded to Cornish stations; these delays were attributed by the South Devon company to delays on the Cornwall Railway.

The passenger traffic continued to expand and in August there was a demand for more station accommodation, especially at Shaugh, the point of access to the Dewerstone area - but passengers had to continue using Bickleigh station for another forty years, as the intermediate stopping place at Shaugh Bridge Platform was not brought into use until 1st August, 1907!

Profit & Loss

From 1860 to 1865 the efforts of the Directors were directed to the efficient running of the company, the provision of additional facilities for dealing with increasing passenger and freight traffic, a revision of the leasing arrangements with the South Devon company so as to maintain the agreed minimum rent received, and the winding up of the Capital Account.

By August 1863 the heaviest account, that of the contractors, had been satisfactorily settled, and amounts due to landowners had been paid up to within a very small amount in respect of which there were counter claims, leaving only about £600 to be paid. The total cost of the line was £248,000.

During its existence as a separate company, the following amounts were paid in interest and dividends: Debenture Interest £7,450; Preference Interest £9,250; Ordinary Dividends £17,800; total £34,500.

The highest dividend was 8s. 9d. per share for the half-year ended 31st December, 1864; the lowest were 2s. 2d. per share for the half-year ended 30th June, 1862, and 2s. 10d. per share for the same period ended 30th June, l863.

In 1862-3 there was a severe financial depression; railway dividends were generally low, and in some cases non-existent. Dividends of the Tavistock company were also affected by improvements for dealing with the increasing traffic put in hand by the South Devon company in 1859-60, involving a capital expenditure of over £250,000. These included doubling of the line Exeter to Starcross; rebuilding of Newton Station; new goods shed at Plymouth; alterations at Ivybridge, and an improved station at Dawlish. They were completed by 1863, and the resulting increase in traffic and revenue was reflected in the dividends paid in the subsequent years. Dividends were also rising on the South Devon, and prospects of a satisfactory amalgamation with that company were attractive.

Amalgamation with the South Devon Railway

It had long been a policy of both companies that they should amalgamate, there being little point keeping independent two concerns, one of which was leased in perpetuity to the other, an arrangement which was inconvenient and expensive. The basis for amalgamation was that terms should be fair and reasonable to both parties, and during 1864 and early in 1865 the question had received much consideration.

The terms finally agreed were for amalgamation between the two parties as from 1st July, 1865, from which date the South Devon & Tavistock proprietors would receive in lieu of the present fluctuating dividends, a fixed guaranteed payment in perpetuity of 17s. 6d. per share per annum, equivalent to £3 10s. per cent per annum.

The arrangements were considered to be satisfactory, and were adopted by the shareholders of both companies in February 1865, but only after an objection from a few of the South Devon shareholders that the terms given to the Tavistock holders were more favourable than the South Devon holders had received. The amalgamation took place as from 1st July, 1865, by virtue of the South Devon Railway Act of 5th July, 1865, Section 22.

The South Devon company in turn became amalgamated with the Great Western Railway Company as from 1st August, 1878, by the GWR and SDR Companies Amalgamation Act of 22nd July, 1878. By this Act the GWR realised, 35 years after their incorporation, their great ambition of becoming truly both 'Great' and 'Western'.

The last meeting of the South Devon & Tavistock company was held on 31st August, 1865. The Tavistock branch had, by that time, been extended to Launceston by the Launceston & South Devon Railway, and it would now be appropriate to examine the history of the Launceston company in greater detail.

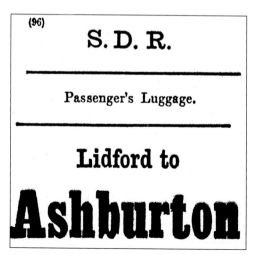

A South Devon Railway luggage label of c. 1870. Note the original spelling of 'Lidford'.

John M. Strange Collection

Chapter Four

Extension to Launceston

Once known by the Celtic name of Dunhevet, Launceston was formerly a place of some importance, being (in years past) the county town of Cornwall and the assize town for a vast rural area stretching as far west as Land's End. In Norman times, its motte and bailey castle symbolised the authority of the Dukes of Cornwall, while in the 13th century the original earth and timber fortifications were rebuilt in more durable stone.

Despite its obvious strategic importance, Launceston occupied a somewhat isolated position around 42 miles from Exeter, 24 from Plymouth, 19 from Bude and Okehampton, 16 from Liskeard and 14 from Holsworthy. The centre of a large agricultural district, embracing twenty-four parishes, it lost much of its importance with the passing of the Reform Act in 1832 when its representation in Parliament was reduced to one Member, and again, six years later, when on 27th August, 1838 the Assizes were transferred to Bodmin and its gaol was closed.

The next twenty years or so saw a continual decline in the trade of the town, and growing isolation as attempts failed to secure a railway.

The district was largely dependent upon the Bude Canal for the conveyance of heavy traffic such as coal, timber, grain and manures.

The Bude Canal Act of 1819 sanctioned this waterway from Bude to Druxton Wharf, four miles from Launceston, a nearer approach to the town being prevented by the Duke of Northumberland, the principal landowner. Earlier attempts had been made for a canal from Bude to the Tamar at Calstock, in 1774, and again in 1795, for a cut from Morwellham to Lamerton bridge with an extension from Poulston bridge near Lifton, to Richgrain Mills near Launceston.

Early Plans

The first railway scheme was in 1836 when an Act was obtained for a harbour at Tremoutha Haven, St Gennys, on the North Cornwall coast between Bude and Boscastle, and for a railway thence to be called the Launceston & Victoria Railway. This failed.

In 1844 the South Devon Railway Company supported Launceston in their proposal for a line to be built on the atmospheric system, to join up with the proposed South Devon scheme at Tavistock. This line was to be about 11 miles long, and would have extended from Tavistock through Mary Tavy, Brentor, Lydford, Coryton, Lamerton, Sydenham Damerel, Milton Abbot, Dunkerton, Bridestowe, Marystowe and Lifton in the County of Devon, and Lawhitton and Lezant, to Launceston in the County of Cornwall.

The estimated cost was about £130,000 one-half of which was to be borne by the South Devon company, who also agreed to lease the line over a period of five years at a rent of 3½ per cent upon the capital involved. Both the

Launceston and the Tavistock schemes came before Parliament in 1845, but were postponed until the following session as the committee required more information about the atmospheric system, about which doubts were then being expressed in Parliament.

By 1846, the North Devon line from Okehampton to Launceston, which was supported by the South Devon Railway, was being considered, and the Launceston promoters altered their route by cutting out the Milton Abbot section and joining up with the North Devon line at Lydford, so as to become part of the proposed trunk line to Launceston. This lengthened the line by about four miles and increased its cost to £200,000.

The failure of the North Devon Bill on Standing Orders caused the failure of both the Launceston and the Tavistock schemes. The Launceston company was dissolved. In view of the subsequent costly failure of the atmospheric system on the South Devon line, it was indeed a blessing in disguise that both the Launceston and the Tavistock projects failed at this particular time.

For many years there was no further move towards bringing a line to the town. Launceston's trade continued to decline, and the town became more and more isolated so far as railway communication was concerned; its population decreased from 6,006 in 1851 to 5,140 just ten years later.

Origins of the Launceston & South Devon Railway

Hopes rose in 1861 when a Bill was proposed for a line from Launceston to Copplestone, there to join the North Devon system from Exeter to Barnstaple; but such hopes were again defeated. This Bill, and other narrow gauge schemes, were supported by the Dukes of Bedford and Northumberland. The South Devon company had no wish to oppose either of these powerful landowners in these promotions, but as they saw in Committee the rival LSWR take up and support the schemes they strongly opposed them and succeeded, on the grounds of insufficiency of the estimates and the unremunerative character of the district through which the line would pass. In examination before the Committee, the Chairman of the South Devon company stated that if the scheme then before Parliament was rejected the South Devon would see that the requirements of Launceston were not overlooked and they would not object to assisting with any future project which the inhabitants of the district were willing to support.

The chance to redeem this pledge came in August 1861 when a meeting was held in Plymouth to consider railway extension in Devon and Cornwall by means of a line from Exeter to Taphouse, near Crediton, thence to Newton via the Teign Valley (a branch which it was claimed would be of great value to the South Devon company). From Taphouse the line would proceed to Okehampton, on to Tavistock and thence to Launceston where it would make a junction with the proposed North Devon line.

This line - the Mid-Devon & Cornwall - would be about 42 miles long, and its estimated cost was so problematical that it was given as 'from £700,000 to £1,000,000'.

Although this expensive scheme did not get much support it had the effect of rousing the South Devon to positive action. This company's line had opened to Tavistock on 22nd June, 1859. It had always been the intention to extend it to Launceston but, as in 1844, the South Devon wished for this to be carried out by an independent company which they would support. Accordingly, the SDR Directors invited six of the prominent townspeople of Launceston to attend a meeting at Plymouth on 24th September, 1861 to hear the views of the South Devon company and to receive proposals. These were favourably accepted by the delegation, who then called a meeting to be held at Launceston on 2nd October, 1861, primarily to put before the public the Mid-Devon & Cornwall scheme which would connect Exeter with Tavistock and Launceston, or to consider a line from Launceston to Tavistock which the South Devon would support.

Public interest was now intense and great excitement and enthusiasm was roused when a notice convening the meeting, and posted in hundreds all over the town, was seen to contain the following exhortation:

Fellow citizens, between these two you will be called upon to decide, but delay not a moment in uniting with the company which will bring you a 'line'. The crisis is one of magnitude and all persons are respectfully requested to attend.

This challenging appeal resulted in a crowded meeting. The Mid-Devon & Cornwall scheme was turned down, and it was agreed that an invitation should be sent to the Directors of the South Devon to attend a meeting to be held at Launceston on 20th October, 1861 to explain in detail their proposals for a line between Tavistock and Launceston. This rather roundabout method of getting Launceston to take the initiative was evidently a matter of policy, and just what the South Devon Directors required.

At the meeting on 20th October, Thomas Woollcombe, Chairman of the South Devon company, explained at great length that the proposal was for a line from Launceston to join the South Devon at Tavistock, the line to be worked by the South Devon at 50 per cent of the total charge on all passenger traffic brought to the South Devon over the Launceston line. Other broad gauge companies would also allow a rebate of 20 per cent on all traffic brought to them over the new line. He thought that the line could be made from £8,000 to £9,000 per mile, and would prove a profitable proposition.

Supporters of the scheme were loud in their appeal for acceptance. They had waited so long for a railway; there had been so many false hopes raised; they had witnessed and heard of the success of communities who had received the benefit of railway communication; had seen the trade and population of their town decline. An air almost of desperation had been created, and the people were urged to accept the offer which would give them a line, even if it was not quite the one they really desired. At this particular moment it was said that ninety per cent of the population were in favour of the scheme which, at last, offered something tangible and had every prospect of success.

The resolution to accept the South Devon offer was carried by a large majority, but there remained a small minority in favour of a narrow gauge line to Exeter, whose clamant voices were to be heard again.

No time was lost in getting on with the scheme. Further meetings took place with the South Devon company and plans were deposited on 30th November, 1861 for a broad gauge line from Launceston to Lydford, passing Lifton, Coryton and Mary Tavy and running thence to Tavistock to form a junction with the South Devon & Tavistock line, a distance of some 19 miles.

The works on the line would be generally light in character; the steepest gradient being 1 in 56 for a distance of about 4 miles between Lydford and Marystowe, which section also had the greatest number of curves, i.e. six, one being of 15 chains. The proposed capital was £180,000, with power to borrow £60,000. The line was planned with a view to extension to the principal parts of the county, and was convenient for a connection with the Central line project, 'if ever it is carried out'. The estimated expenditure included an amount of £5,706 for a tunnel through the estate of Sydenham, as the owner, Mr Tremayne, objected to the sight of a train passing his house at a distance of 340 yards. Objections were also raised by Mr Bradshaw of Lifton Park, on the grounds of residential injury, and by the Dukes of Bedford and Northumberland, the principal landowners.

The Struggle in Parliament

The Launceston Bill appeared before the Committee of the House of Commons on 13th and 14th March, 1862, when the case for the promoters was heard. Counsel for the company were in the happy position of being able to announce that the Duke of Bedford had decided only a day or so before, not only to withdraw his objection, but to support the scheme by giving the land required in exchange for shares, and the Duke of Northumberland, in response to a petition signed by over 700 of the inhabitants of Launceston within a short space of 24 hours, had withdrawn his objection and contributed £5,000 towards the scheme.

On Monday, 17th March Lord Palmerston, the Prime Minister, was called for the opposition and supported, as a general policy, the narrow gauge system for connecting the principal arsenals and military ports of the country, and in particular the proposal for an inland line to Devonport, as the existing broad gauge line so near to the coast was vulnerable and liable to interruption from the landing of enemy forces. He admitted, however, in cross examination, that the provision in the Bill compelling the company to lay down the narrow gauge should another narrow gauge line wish to connect with it, would render the scheme less objectionable, and further stated that he had not been aware of such a provision. After further evidence, the Commissioners announced their unanimous approval of the preamble of the Bill.

This initial success in the passage of the Bill was immediately telegraphed to Tavistock station, and taken by mounted courier to Launceston, who, 'although his horse threw a shoe as he came through the South Gate, never halted until he reached the White Hart, where he announced the glad tidings'. This sparked off a display of excitement and enthusiasm unparalleled in the town's history. Bells were rung; the town band played; there were bonfires in the streets, and all business was suspended for the day. On the following day a whole holiday was given to the school children, and there were great rejoicings.

But the Bill still had to come before the Upper House. To assist its passage, a meeting was held on 23rd April, 1862, as a result of which, a petition, twenty yards long, signed by over two thousand of the inhabitants of Launceston and district, was sent to Westminster and presented on 15th May, 1862. Three days later, Mr Tremayne withdrew his opposition to the line passing through his property thus saving the company the sum of £5,706.

In May 1862, Mr Bradshaw, one of the chief opponents, made overtures to the promoters to abandon his position, provided that his expenses were reimbursed. He was informed that 'not one farthing should be paid, but if it was desired that the line through Lifton Park should be deviated slightly, or the station at Lifton be altered as to position, the Committee would accede to it.'

Mr Bradshaw evidently took this advice, for when the Bill came before the House of Lords on 4th June, 1862, he submitted an alternative scheme to carry the line through his property, within the limits of deviation, on the other side of the River Tamar, thus avoiding the level crossings to which he had so much objected. The last obstacle having been removed, the Lords were able to pass the Launceston & South Devon Railway Bill, which became an Act on 30th June, 1862.

The resulting Act provided consent for a railway commencing at Tavistock by a junction with the South Devon & Tavistock line, and terminating at Launceston, a distance of 19 miles. To pay for this line the promoters were authorised to issue capital of £180,000 in ten pound shares, with a further £60,000 by loan.

The South Devon Railway would work the line, when completed, in return for a share in the gross receipts, and there were arrangements whereby the Great Western and other broad gauge companies would allow rebates on certain categories of traffic.

A further Bill was presented in the 1863 session of Parliament to give effect to the agreed diversion. This was between Lifton and Coryton stations, and commenced about 1¼ miles east of the point where Lifton station was subsequently built. It was 1 mile 52½ chains long and carried the line about a quarter of a mile, to the north of the original course, thus avoiding two crossings of the river Lyd, which had to be slightly diverted in two places. A public road also had to be altered at one point. The new course included a proposed tunnel 506 yards long at a depth of 63 ft 6 in. from ground level to crown of the arch, but this was avoided by substituting a cutting.

Construction and Opening of the Launceston Line

Immediate steps were taken to carry out the provisions of the Launceston & South Devon Act. Peter John Margary (1820-1896) was appointed Engineer with John Fowler (1817-1898) as Consulting Engineer. Both men had already carried out much work on the GWR and its constituents; P.J. Margary, for example, was the South Devon Engineer, while John Fowler had worked for both the Oxford Worcester & Wolverhampton Railway and the GWR itself. Mr Yorks was selected as contractor, and the contract was signed on 29th April, 1863.

The work soon started and progress was eagerly watched, first from Lydford to Coryton, then on to Lifton and Launceston. The placing into position of girders across the Tamar at Poulston and the appearance of the first engine on its trial run, were great occasions.

By May 1865 the Directors had been assured that the line would be ready for a formal opening on 29th May but, as this was a Monday, a day generally inconvenient, it was decided that the opening should be on 1st June. Accordingly, on this date, a special train of 14 coaches left Plymouth at 10.45 am, worked by two South Devon ' Hawk' class engines, *Dart* and *Giraffe*.

At Tavistock the train was greeted by a band of the Royal Marines playing on the platform; another coach was attached, and the train left at 11.50 am. Upon arrival at Launceston, the usual address of welcome was read, and the rest of the day was given up to celebrations, which were carried out in spite of incessant rain. The school children had been given a full day's holiday, and the next day only 15 attended school, the rest apparently had not recovered from the drenching.

A month elapsed, however, before the line was opened to the public; the delay was due to an unusual circumstance, a second inspection of the line being necessary before the Board of Trade would issue their certificate. Colonel Yolland, the Inspecting Officer, made his first inspection on Monday, 12th June, 1865. He was highly pleased with the construction, but stated 'there were a few little things to be done before the line could, with safety, be opened for traffic'. These included some unfinished fences, but he did not consider that a second inspection by him would be necessary; instead, it was arranged that P.J. Margary, the Engineer, should see that all was put in order and certify accordingly to the Board of Trade.

Mr Margary made his inspection on 19th June, went to London the same night and reported to the Board on Wednesday, 21st June. The Board accepted

A view northwards along the broad gauge trackwork at Tavistock in 1865; note the bridge rails and longitudinal sleepers.   *S.E. Wootton*

Mr Margary's report and said they were quite satisfied with his inspection, but at the same time they held Colonel Yolland responsible. He, however, felt he could not accept responsibility for an inspection he had not made, and, decided to go over the line again. On Saturday, 24th June, 1865, he arrived at Tavistock by special Inspection train, and at once proceeded over the line to Launceston. He found everything to his satisfaction, and the line was publicly opened on the following Saturday, 1st July, 1865.

Some Details of the Launceston Line

The new railway was a single track, broad gauge branch, extending from the South Devon & Tavistock station at Tavistock to Launceston; the line followed a somewhat circuitous course, running first due north along the valley of the Tavy, and then swinging westwards via the Lyd valley. The chosen route did, however, obviate the need for major bridge works, and there were no tunnels or viaducts on the 19 mile Launceston & South Devon line.

Intermediate stations were provided from the outset at Mary Tavy, Lydford, Coryton and Lifton. Each of these stopping places was provided with a small, but substantially-built station building, while the terminal station at Launceston was equipped with a relatively large range of stone buildings; these distinctive structures had probably been designed by P.J. Margary, the line's Engineer.

All train services were provided by the South Devon Railway, and the initial train service comprised five trains each weekday between Plymouth and Launceston, with four in the reverse direction and two workings each way on Sundays. The line was worked, in effect, as an extension of the original line from Plymouth, with trains running through to Plymouth via Tavistock, Horrabridge and Bickleigh.

The operating agreement arranged between the South Devon Railway and the Launceston & South Devon company provided that the South Devon Railway would take fifty per cent of the revenue for working the line, and that the Launceston company should also receive by way of rebate twenty five per cent of all receipts on passenger traffic brought to the South Devon Railway over the Launceston line, and twenty per cent of like receipts on traffic to other broad gauge lines, i.e. the Great Western, Bristol & Exeter, Cornwall, and West Cornwall companies.

This meant that the Launceston company had to support themselves out of their own net earnings, and it was a great relief when the first year's traffic returns showed that 95,193 passengers and 18,997 tons of traffic had been carried and the net revenue was sufficient to pay every charge upon revenue account such as debenture, preference, and establishment charges, salaries, rates, taxes and income tax, and provide a balance which, instead of being used to pay a dividend, was carried forward to help defray capital expenditure and so reduce the deficit on capital account.

This pattern was followed until the half-year ended 31st December, 1869, when the balances of accumulated half-yearly surplus were used to declare a maiden dividend of 15s. per cent on the ordinary share capital.

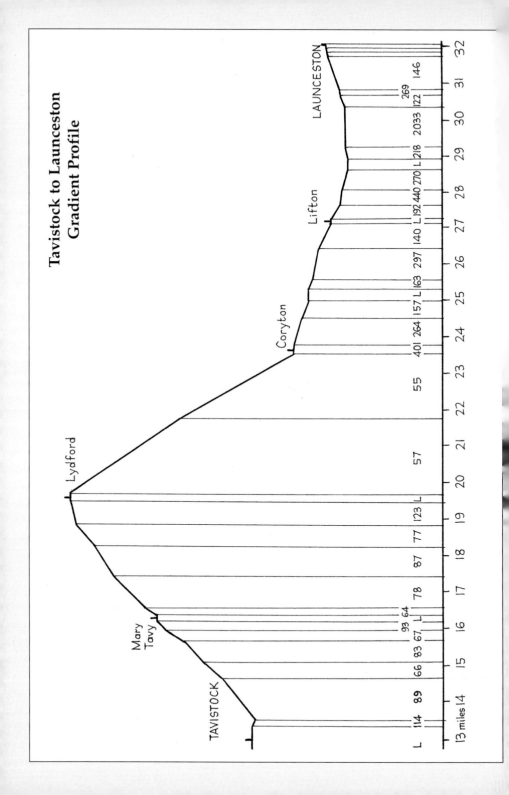

Tavistock to Launceston
Gradient Profile

Later History of the Launceston Company

As will be seen from the following details, traffic, especially goods traffic, continued to expand, and half-yearly dividends showed moderate increases up to the half-year ended 30th June, 1873, when the highest dividend (2 per cent) was available for distribution.

Period	Number of Passengers	Goods, Tons	Net Earnings
1865-66	95,193	18,997	£4,932
1866-67	92,985	27,730	£5,270
1867-68	86,799	not available	£5,487
1868-69	87,000	29,022	£5,608
1869-70	89,960	33,832	£6,161
1870-71	not available	not available	not available
1871-72	96,937	38,483	£6,609
1872-73	114,590	41,297	not available

From 1865 to amalgamation, the Directors were fully engaged in improving handling facilities at stations, in dealing with the complex capital situation, in pressing the South Devon Railway for a better train service and arranging the amalgamation terms.

During the first winter, 1865-6, the line endured a most severe test when there was extensive flooding which inundated several miles of track, but which, fortunately, caused no serious interference with traffic or any derailments, and the Directors were happy to be able to congratulate the contractor on the soundness of the work generally.

In August 1866, the engineer reported that the works had been efficiently maintained and were in a satisfactory condition. A siding had been put in between Mary Tavy and Lydford for the convenience of farmers and traders in the Brentor area, and accommodation was being improved where necessary to assist the developing goods traffic.

In 1870 a new goods station was erected at Lifton at a cost of £150, and the South Devon were considering the covering of Launceston station, which had provided the passengers with 'the most exceptional facilities for getting drenched'.

Launceston was the largest and busiest station on the new line. Its goods traffic increased steadily with culm, lime, coal, grain, timber and livestock contributing a large share.

Culm, a small coal used in the lime kilns, was unloaded for as little as 2*d*. per ton, but lime traffic cost 1*s*. 1*d*. per bushel to unload. Lime was used in large quantities by North Cornwall farmers in the early days until the price at the kilns was increased by one shilling per ton; the farmers then made increasing use of sea-sand as a fertiliser.

Coal traffic was heavy, and the company was able to fend off severe competition by the Bude Canal Company which had developed by 1869. By the latter year Launceston market had 'become superior to Tavistock market', and it was claimed that the town afforded a remarkable example of the advantages of railway communication.

Trade had increased in every direction, business premises which had closed during the lean years re-opened, and within a few years this Cornish town regained its old position as 'Metropolis of the north of Cornwall and adjacent parts of Devon'. Prices were cheaper; coal, for instance, being £1 1s. per ton at Launceston station compared with £1 6s. 8d. per ton before the opening of the line.

There still remained resentment at the poor train service which had given 'the insignificant town of Tavistock' five trains daily compared with Launceston's three. On the other hand, the opening of the Launceston & South Devon line had clearly given the traders and residents of Launceston a vital rail link to the outside world, and although the town's population continued to decline throughout the 19th century, the situation would clearly have been much worse if the railway had never been built; to that extent, it could be argued that the coming of the railway succeeded in arresting the economic decline of Launceston and the surrounding area - although the overall benefits were not as great as the railway's promoters would perhaps have expected.

The End of Local Control

The Launceston branch had been constructed under the auspices of a nominally independent company, but it was always assumed that, in the fullness of time, the local company would become part of the parent South Devon company.

In the event, absorption came sooner rather than later, and the Launceston & South Devon Railway was vested in the South Devon company by an Act obtained on 24th June, 1869; this Act also created £33,500 worth of debenture stock, wherewith the Launceston company was relieved of its liabilities. This was not quite the end of the story, for final amalgamation did not take place until 31st December, 1873. Finally, the entire South Devon system passed into Great Western ownership on 1st August, 1878, and the branch line to Launceston thereby became an appendage of the mighty GWR empire.

The Acts of Parliament for the Launceston & South Devon Railway Company were:

Act of Incorporation, 30th June, 1862
For making a deviation, etc., 29th June, 1863
Further powers relating to capital, 28th June, 1866
Enlargements of powers for raising money and vesting the undertaking in the South Devon Railway, 24th June, 1869

Chapter Five

The London & South Western Invasion
& Other Developments

The LSWR invasion of the West can be said to have begun as far back as 1832, for it was in that year that the Bodmin & Wadebridge Railway was sanctioned. It opened on 4th July, 1834, and despite its remoteness from London, this minor Cornish line became an important factor in the great struggle which was to go on for some 60 years between the Great Western and the London & South Western railways for supremacy in the West.

The Battle of the Gauges

The Battle of the Gauges in the far west of England started in 1844 with the Great Western Railway sponsoring the broad gauge South Devon and the Cornwall Railways, and the London & South Western backing the Cornwall & Devon Central scheme, first mooted in 1835 and revived ten years later, for a narrow gauge line from Exeter through Crediton, Okehampton, Launceston and Bodmin, to Truro and Falmouth.

In 1845, the Cornwall Railway offered to buy the Bodmin & Wadebridge Railway provided its own Act of incorporation was obtained. The rival Cornwall & Devon company offered to do the same, whether they obtained their Act or not. The Bodmin & Wadebridge company accepted the offer of £33,096 9s. 8d. made by the latter company, who, however, failed to obtain their Act. The London & South Western Railway then stepped in and acquired the line for the sum named, although at the time the line was some 120 miles away from the rest of the LSWR system. This remote and insignificant railway was to be a source of embarrassment to the Great Western but one of inspiration to the London & South Western for the next 50 years, which was the time it took the latter company to link up with its far-off outpost.

Meanwhile, the London & South Western company was gradually extending its influence westwards. Its line between Yeovil and Exeter Queen Street, opened on 19th July, 1860, was extended to Exeter St David's on 1st February, 1862, and the mixed gauge through that station was then carried through to Cowley Bridge Junction. At Cowley Bridge, LSWR trains reached the mixed gauge trackwork of the Exeter & Crediton Railway, and by this means the South Western company was able to extend its 4 ft 8½ in. gauge services through to Barnstaple and Bideford - standard gauge communication being established throughout to the latter place via the mixed gauge of the Exeter & Crediton and North Devon railways on 1st March, 1863.

In 1862, the Okehampton Railway company was authorised to construct a line from Coleford Junction, 77 chains west of Yeoford Junction, to Okehampton, which was opened in the following stages: Coleford Junction to North Tawton, 6 miles 77 chains, on 1st November, 1865; North Tawton to Okehampton Road (later Belstone Corner, and later still, Sampford Courtenay),

2 miles 65 chains, on 8th January, 1867; Okehampton Road to Okehampton, 3 miles 55 chains, on 3rd October, 1871. The name of the Okehampton company was subsequently changed to the Devon & Cornwall Railway Company. This company, backed by the London & South Western, obtained powers in 1863 to extend their line from Okehampton to Lydford, a distance of 9 miles 73 chains.

The powers granted, in spite of strong opposition from the Great Western company, placed an obligation on the South Devon Railway to lay mixed gauge on the line from Lydford to Plymouth as and when requested by the Devon & Cornwall company, to enable narrow gauge trains to run through to Plymouth. By the time the Okehampton line had been opened on 12th October, 1874, the Devon & Cornwall company had been taken over by the London & South Western, which then called upon the South Devon company to honour the agreement and lay mixed track so that narrow gauge trains could be extended to Plymouth.

The LSWR Reaches Tavistock

The London & South Western company was fully supported by the people of Tavistock and the surrounding districts. Although the area was served by the existing broad gauge line from Plymouth to Launceston, many local people believed that the stimulus of extra competition would lead to much improved transport facilities. Accordingly, in the early part of November 1874, the Portreeve of the Court Leet and Court Baron of Tavistock, in compliance with a requisition, convened a public meeting in Tavistock Town Hall for:

. . . the purpose of taking such measures as may appear to be desirable to prevail upon the London & South Western company to run their trains through to Tavistock and to make that station their terminus until the Plymouth extension of the narrow gauge is completed, and thereby to remedy the great inconvenience that arises to the district generally by the narrow gauge trains stopping at Lidford. Also to take into consideration the desirability of rendering assistance to the South Western company to obtain an independent station at the east end of the town, it being understood that the company is desirous of such accommodation.

A contemporary report states that the meeting was well attended. One prominent citizen pointed out that the narrow gauge route was fifty miles shorter to London and twenty-nine miles shorter to Exeter, adding that the South Western company, by putting on a road coach to Okehampton had given the people of Tavistock cheap and quick trains to London.

There was clearly a groundswell of popular opinion in favour of bringing the London & South Western line into Tavistock, and at the end of the meeting it was unanimously resolved that:

. . . the Portreeve having received a letter from the Directors of the South Western Company stating that they were willing to run their trains from Lidford to Tavistock, the South Devon Company be requested to grant the necessary facilities for carrying out this object as soon as possible, and that should the Directors of the South Devon

Company be unwilling to grant such facilities, the London & South Western Company be most urgently asked to take the necessary measures to compel the South Devon Company to give access to the narrow gauge trains from Tavistock.

It was also reported that the Duke of Bedford had given an undertaking that he would give every facility for getting for Tavistock the best railway accommodation.

The Portreeve had considerable correspondence with both the Directors of the London & South Western and the South Devon companies. Both said they were in touch with each other, but it soon became evident that there was no prospect of the suggestion being adopted.

By November 1874 the narrow gauge lines between the two stations at Lydford were unfinished, and on 15th February, 1875, the South Devon company wrote that after asking the London & South Western to state their requirements, they had at last received a reply indicating their needs at the two stations, but they had received no application from the London & South Western company to run their trains through Tavistock in anticipation of their coming through from Lydford to Plymouth and Devonport. In fact, the position was that their works were, as yet, far from completion.

This ended the correspondence, and the people of Tavistock had to wait until 17th May, 1876 before the first South Western train arrived at the Tavistock station of the South Devon Railway. This event was welcomed with great public rejoicing at Devonport, and to a lesser degree, but just as warmly, at Tavistock.

The special train for the official opening left Queen Street, Exeter at 11.15 am. It consisted of seven saloons and first-class carriages and two brake vans, and was drawn by one of the company's most powerful engines.

The journey from Exeter occupied two hours 50 minutes, including stoppages at Crediton, Yeoford Junction and North Tawton. At the latter station the party had to await the arrival of the first train from Devonport, the new London & South Western terminus. This train, drawn by a 'Gem' class engine, was gaily decorated. The Directors' train then proceeded to Okehampton and Lydford. There was a stay of five minutes at the latter station during which the South Devon Traffic Manager, Mr Compton, joined the inaugural train.

The next stop was at Tavistock. Although the town was not decorated and the reception was of a hurried nature, some hundreds of people had assembled outside the station and the Portreeve was able to deliver an address of welcome to the narrow gauge system which brought them 54 miles nearer the Metropolis.

At Mutley station, the next stop, the South Devon officials detrained. The train then proceeded to North Road station, where the South Western company reached its own property.

The first journey was then made 'over the virgin rails' to Devonport, where there was a tremendous reception, the band of the Dockyard and Keyham Artillery playing *The Conquering Hero*. The engine which brought the train in was decorated with flags and flowers and bore a headboard with the words: 'Many thanks for your kind welcome'.

The Plymouth Devonport & South Western Junction Railway

Although the London & South Western Railway had gained an entry into Plymouth, it was possible only over their competitor's route, and the arrangement proved by no means satisfactory. The additional traffic meant intense occupation of a single line laid with the mixed gauge. Delays were frequent, and it was generally felt that the Great Western company (who by this time had acquired the South Devon) gave their own trains some degree of preference.

This was not looked upon very kindly by the people of Plymouth, and as a result a Bill was presented to Parliament in 1882 on their behalf, in which it was proposed that an independent line would be constructed alongside the Great Western track between Lydford and Plymouth to accommodate the London & South Western trains.

Despite strong opposition from the Great Western the Bill was authorised by both Houses of Parliament in the same year. The proposal was, however, abandoned in favour of the Plymouth, Devonport & South Western Junction scheme, the Act for which was passed on 25th August, 1883, and the South Western ceased to use the Great Western line when this direct route to Plymouth via Okehampton, Tavistock and Bere Alston was opened on 2nd June, 1890. Both companies were doubtless glad to terminate an arrangement which had done nothing to improve relations between them.

The LSWR Reaches Launceston

As was the case with Tavistock, the people of Launceston were not content to be served only by the broad gauge interest, and many attempts were made to bring the narrow gauge to the town.

In 1864 the Launceston, Bodmin & Wadebridge Railway was incorporated, with power to make arrangements with the Okehampton company, but after the company had obtained another Act changing its name to the Central Railway company with permission to extend to Truro, the scheme was abandoned. In 1873 the Devon & Cornwall company secured an Act for an extension to Holsworthy and Camelford, and to Launceston and the South Devon line, but this, too, fell through.

In 1872 when the Devon & Cornwall company gave notice to lay a narrow gauge line between Lydford and Tavistock, it was suggested at the Launceston company's half-yearly meeting held on 24th February that the South Devon should be asked that the third rail be extended from Lydford to Launceston, but the majority felt they owed so much to the South Devon for supporting their scheme for a railway that it would not be proper for them to be asked to agree to such a proposal. This was indeed a case of altruism which was noticeably rare among the hard-headed businessmen of the age.

Five years later, however, a different attitude prevailed and another effort, almost of desperation, was made when the people of Launceston held a meeting attended by one of the Railway Commissioners and resolved to ask for the mixed gauge to be extended to Launceston. Although the matter was pressed the Great Western company, who now owned the line, were not encouraging, and the matter lapsed.

It was not until 25th July, 1886 that the narrow gauge reached the town from Halwill Junction, when a line, 13⅚ miles in length, was finally opened through to Launceston.

Later History of the Launceston Line

Reverting to the history of the Great Western route from Plymouth to Launceston, it would now be convenient to sketch-in some further details relating to developments during the late 19th and early 20th centuries. As we have seen, the Launceston company passed into South Devon ownership under Powers obtained in 1869, and in 1878 the South Devon Railway was itself absorbed by the Great Western Railway.

Great Western ownership did not in itself lead to any major changes on the Launceston branch - the most important developments during the 1880s being associated with the LSWR, rather than the Great Western company. There were, nevertheless, one or two significant events during the later years of the 19th century, notably the opening of the Princetown branch on 11th August, 1883 and the narrowing of the gauge between Plymouth and Launceston in May 1892.

The story of the Princetown branch will be told in detail in *Chapter Nine*, suffice to say that, when first opened, there was no junction station at Yelverton, and Princetown branch trains therefore ran through to Horrabridge for connecting purposes. This situation was amended on 1st May, 1885, when a new junction station was opened at Yelverton, between Bickleigh and Horrabridge.

The Plymouth to Launceston branch was converted to the standard gauge of 4 ft 8½ in. on the weekend of 20th-22nd May, 1892 - all GWR lines west of Exeter being narrowed at that time in one gigantic engineering operation. As mentioned above, standard gauge LSWR trains had used the line between Lydford and Marsh Mills from 1876 until 1890, mixed 7 ft and 4 ft 8½ in. gauge trackwork being provided between those two places. Standard gauge trains had never before worked between Lydford and Launceston, however, and in this respect the gauge conversion that took place in May 1892 was clearly an event of some significance.

Further changes took place during the 1890s and early 1900s when the characteristic 'Brunelian' timber viaducts at Cann Woods, Riverford, Bickleigh, Ham Green, Horrabridge (Magpie) and Walkham were progressively rebuilt in more durable materials. These structures had lasted for many years, but sadly, it became increasingly difficult to obtain timber of the necessary quality, and with repair work becoming ever more expensive these six viaducts were all rebuilt at intervals - the first two to be dealt with being Riverford and Bickleigh viaducts, which were both replaced by masonry viaducts on 12th March, 1893.

Ham Green Viaduct was replaced on 19th November, 1899, while Magpie

Whit-Monday, May 30th.

UP TRAINS.

STATIONS.		No. 1 Empty G.W.N.G. Engine.	No. 2 Train N.G.	No. 3 Train N.G.	No. 4 Train B.G.	No. 5 Train N.G.	No. 6 Train N.G.
		A.M.	A.M.	A.M.	P.M.	P.M.	P.M.
Devonport (L. & S. W. R.) ...	dep.	7 0	8 0	11 0		2 40	7 25
Plymouth ...	"	—	8 10	11 5	1 20	2 45	7 31
North Road ...	"	—	8 11	11 7	1 26	2 47	7 33
Mutley ...	"				1 29		
Marsh Mills ...	"	STAFF 7 11	TICKET X8 16	TICKET X11 13	STAFF 1 36	TICKET 2 53	STAFF 7 40
Bickleigh ...	"	STAFF X7 34	STAFF 8 25	STAFF 11 24	STAFF X1 50	STAFF 3 4	STAFF 7 50
Yelverton ...	"	X7 42	STAFF 8 34	TICKET X11 35	TICKET X2 1	TICKET X3 14	TICKET X7 59
Horrabridge ...	"		TICKET X8 39	TICKET 11 40	TICKET 2 8	STAFF 3 19	STAFF 8 5
Tavistock ...	"		STAFF 8 48	TICKET 11 50	2 16	TICKET X3 29	STAFF X8 18
Mary Tavy ...	"		STAFF 8 56	TICKET 11 58		TICKET 3 37	STAFF X8 31
Lidford ...	arr.		9 4	12 5		3 45	XX8 39

The examination of Tickets at Tavistock and Mary Tavy on Whit-Monday will be suspended. Lidford to collect their own Tickets.

No. 1 Empty N.G. G.W. Engine will cross—X 6.47 a.m. L. & S.W. Goods at Bickleigh.
X 7.7 a.m. Yelverton.
The 8.35 p.m. Up G.W. Train of **Sunday Night** must take a Ticket Marsh Mills to Bickleigh.

No. 2 Train will cross—X The 7.7 a.m. N.G. Goods Train at Marsh Mills.
X The 7.40 a.m. Down L. & S.W. Goods must take the Staff Yelverton to Bickleigh.
Bickleigh to Horrabridge.

REMARK.—The 7.40 a.m. Up N.G. Passenger Train must take a Ticket instead of a Staff, Bickleigh to Horrabridge.

No. 3 Train will cross—X The 10.15 a.m. N.G. Passenger Train at Marsh Mills.
X The 10.30 a.m. N.G. Passenger Train at Yelverton.

REMARKS.—The 10.15 a.m. Down N.G. Train must take the Staff Yelverton to Bickleigh.

No. 4 Train will cross—X The 1.11 p.m. Down N.G. Passenger Train at Bickleigh.
X The 12.55 p.m. Down N.G. Goods Train at Yelverton.

REMARKS.—The 11.43 a.m. Up N.G. Train must take a Ticket Marsh Mills to Bickleigh.
X The 1.11 p.m. Down N.G. Train must take the Staff Yelverton to Bickleigh.

No. 5 Train will cross—X The 2.5 p.m. G.W. Passenger Train at Yelverton.
X The 2.47 p.m. Up N.G. Passenger Train at Mary Tavy.

REMARKS.—The 2.30 p.m. Up B.G. Train must take a Ticket Bickleigh to Yelverton, and Horrabridge to Tavistock.

No. 6 Train will cross—X The 7.25 p.m. N.G. Special ex Lidford at Yelverton.
X The 8.4 p.m. N.G. Passenger Train at Tavistock.
X The 8.28 p.m. N.G. Down Passenger Train at Mary Tavy.
X The 6.50 p.m. B.G. Goods Train at Lidford.
The 8.10 p.m. B.G. Passenger Train at Lidford.

REMARKS.—The 8.4 p.m. N.G. Train must take the Staff from Mary Tavy to Tavistock.
The 8.28 p.m. N.G. Train must take the Staff from Lidford to Mary Tavy.

Whit-Monday, May 30th.

DOWN TRAINS.

STATIONS.		No. 1 Train N.G.	No. 2 Train N.G.	No. 3 Train B.G.	No. 4 Train N.G.	No. 5 Train N.G.
		A.M.	P.M.	P.M.	P.M.	P.M.
Lidford ...	dep.	STAFF 9 22	TICKET 4 45		STAFF 7 25	TICKET 10 20
Mary Tavy ...	"	TICKET X9 32	STAFF 4 54		X7 34	10 30
Tavistock ...	"	STAFF 9 40	TICKET X5 10	STAFF 6 30	X7 46	10 43
Horrabridge ...	"	STAFF 9 50	STAFF 5 20	STAFF X6 45	STAFF 7 54	10 52
Yelverton ...	"	STAFF 9 54	TICKET X5 27	TICKET X6 55	TICKET X7 58	10 57
Bickleigh ...	"	STAFF 10 8	STAFF 5 38	STAFF 7 4	STAFF 8 6	STAFF 11 6
Marsh Mills ...	"	TICKET 10 18	STAFF 5 49	STAFF 7 14	STAFF 8 16	11 16
Mutley ...	"	TICKET 10 24	STAFF 5 54	STAFF 7 22	STAFF 8 25	11 20
North Road ...	"	TICKET 10 26	TICKET 5 57	STAFF 7 26	STAFF 8 28	11 23
Plymouth ...	arr.					
Devonport (L. & S. W. R.) ...	arr.	10 30	6 2		8 32	11 27

The examination of Tickets at Coryton and Marsh Mills will be suspended on Whit-Monday. Lidford to collect their own Tickets.

Cattle must not be sent by Passenger Trains on Whit-Monday.

THE 7.40 A.M. DOWN TRAIN TO BE WORKED WITH A GOODS ENGINE. Mr. SAMPSON to arrange.

No. 1 Train will cross—X The 8.23 a.m. B.G. Passenger Train at Mary Tavy.
The 7.40 a.m. Down Train must take the Staff Bickleigh to Marsh Mills.

REMARKS.—The 8.23 a.m. B.G. Passenger Train must take the Staff Bickleigh to Yelverton.

No. 2 Train will cross—X The 3.35 p.m. Up N.G. Goods Train at Tavistock.
X The 4.50 p.m. Up N.G. Passenger Train at Yelverton.

REMARKS.—The 3.35 p.m. Up N.G. Goods Train must take the Staff Horrabridge to Tavistock.
The 4.21 p.m. Down N.G. Passenger Train must take a Ticket Mary Tavy to Tavistock, and Horrabridge to Yelverton.

No. 3 Train will cross—X The 5.55 p.m G.W Passenger Train at Horrabridge.
X The 6.0 p.m. Up N.G. Goods Train at Yelverton.

REMARKS.—The 5.54 p.m. Down N.G. Train must take a Ticket Tavistock to Horrabridge.
The 5.55 p.m. Up B.G. Train must take the Staff Yelverton to Horrabridge.
The 6.0 p.m. Up N.G. Goods must take the Staff Marsh Mills to Bickleigh.

No. 4 Train will cross—X The 6.0 p.m. Up N.G. Goods Train at Mary Tavy.
X The 7.0 p.m. Up N.G. Passenger Train at Tavistock.
X The 7.25 p.m. Up N.G. Special Train at Yelverton.

REMARKS.—The 6.0 p.m. Up N.G. Goods Train must take the Staff from Tavistock to Mary Tavy.
The 5.55 p.m. Up B.G. Train must take the Staff Mary Tavy to Lidford.
The 7.0 p.m. Up N.G. Train must take a Ticket Bickleigh to Yelverton.
The 6.5 p.m. Up N.G. Goods Train must take a Ticket Bickleigh to Marsh Mills.

No. 5 Train—The 5.50 p.m. G.W. Goods Train must take a Ticket Bickleigh to Marsh Mills.

A special traffic notice for Whit-Monday trains showing broad gauge and 'narrow gauge' trains. The date of this document is uncertain, it was issued in either 1881 or 1887.

C.R. Potts Collection

Viaduct was superseded on 8th June, 1902. The Cann Viaduct was replaced on 10th March, 1907 and finally, in September 1910, the mighty Walkham Viaduct was replaced by a new structure consisting of girder spans resting on masonry piers (*see also Chapter Seven*).

The removal of these timber viaducts was a necessary, though regrettable development on the Tavistock and Launceston branch. A somewhat happier innovation concerned the opening of three new stopping places to cater for growing residential and tourist traffic. These were at Plym Bridge, Whitchurch Down and Shaugh Bridge, and they were opened on 1st May, 1906, 1st September, 1906, and 19th August, 1907 respectively.

In 1923 the London & South Western Railway was amalgamated with the London Brighton & South Coast Railway, the South Eastern & Chatham Railway (and other companies) to form a new, enlarged organisation known as the Southern Railway. The 1923 grouping did not, however, have much effect on the Great Western which absorbed several English and Welsh lines but was otherwise unaffected by the 1922/23 amalgamations.

In the next few years the Great Western and Southern companies introduced several small, but useful cost-cutting measures - though both companies continued to maintain entirely separate lines between Lydford and Plymouth; similarly, at Launceston, the two companies retained separate stations which could (sensibly) have been replaced by one jointly-owned establishment. Only at Lydford, where the Great Western had withdrawn its staff during World War I, did the GWR and SR companies make any real attempt at rationalisation of facilities.

There were, on the other hand, much closer operational links between the two systems during World War II. The railways were (as in World War I) taken into government control for the duration of hostilities, and in this situation a running link was re-established at Lydford and a new connecting line was installed between the Great Western and Southern lines at Launceston. These connecting lines were both brought into use in 1943, and both will be referred to in greater detail in *Chapter Eight*.

The Great Western had, meanwhile, continued to open new halts for local travellers on the Launceston route, Clearbrook Halt (between Shaugh Bridge Platform and Yelverton) being opened on 29th October, 1928, while Liddaton Halt (between Lydford and Coryton) was opened to public traffic on 4th April, 1938.

Liddaton Halt was destined to be the last stopping place opened on the Launceston branch, which had 15 stations by the end of the Great Western era. These stations varied tremendously in terms of traffic facilities, some being fully equipped stations with a wide range of facilities for passenger and goods traffic, while others were merely unstaffed, passenger-only halts. Launceston and Tavistock, for instance, were equipped with goods sheds, yard cranes, loading banks, cattle pens and end-loading docks for machinery, motor cars or other wheeled road vehicles. Yelverton, in contrast, was primarily a passenger station (though it had limited goods facilities) and Shaugh Bridge, Clearbrook and the other halts had no goods facilities whatsoever.

The following table, compiled with reference to the 1938 Railway Clearing

House *Handbook of Stations*, shows the various stations and halts *en route* to Launceston, with details of the goods facilities at each location.

Although a key is given at the end of the table, it may be worth adding that the latter 'L' indicates that the stations concerned had cattle loading pens, while the presence of 'H' or 'C' shows that loading docks were available for the shipment of horses or carriage traffic. Carriages or other vehicles were invariably loaded in end-loading bays, GWR 'motor car vans' having end doors through which road vehicles could be driven under their own power.

Fixed hand cranes were provided only at the larger stations, though rail-mounted cranes could be sent to wayside stations if loads of timber or other heavy consignments were sent by rail.

Goods & Passenger Accommodation on the Tavistock & Launceston Line, 1938

Station	m	ch	Facilities	Crane	Notes
Marsh Mills	00	18	G P	-	Various sidings
Plym Bridge Platform	01	39	P	-	
Bickleigh	04	09	G P L L H	-	
Shaugh Bridge Platform	04	79	P	-	
Clearbrook Halt	06	25	P	-	
Yelverton	07	37	P L H	-	
Horrabridge	08	77	G P L H	3 ton 5 cwt	
Whitchurch Down Halt	11	65	P	-	
Tavistock	12	71	G P F L H C	6 tons	Pitts Cleave Siding
					Gas Works Siding
Mary Tavy	16	23	G P	-	
Lydford	19	43	G P F L H C	-	
Liddaton Halt	22	35	P	-	
Coryton	23	76	G P F L	-	
Lifton	27	14	G P F L H C	6 tons	Bryley's Siding
					Leat Mill Siding
					Cawdron Quarry Siding
Launceston	31	64	G P F L H C	7 tons 10 cwt	

G = Goods traffic; P = Passenger station; F = Furniture vans, motor cars, etc; L = Livestock traffic; H = Horses & Prize cattle vans; C = Carriages, etc

The position regarding private sidings is confusing in that some sidings had a comparatively short life, while others were added in the 20th century; Cawdron quarry siding (near Lifton) for example, had fallen out of use by the turn-of-the-century, whereas Tavistock gas works sidings was not opened until 1938. For this reason, the table does not include a full list of all private sidings, and readers seeking further information on the industrial lines at Marsh Mills, Tavistock and elsewhere should refer to *Chapter Seven* and *Chapter Eight*, both of which contain much further information relating to the private sidings between Marsh Mills and Launceston.

Chapter Six

Train Working and Other Details

Little has been said so far regarding the operation of the Tavistock and Launceston branch, and the following chapter will therefore provide details of train services, motive power and other operational matters.

Train Services

When the line to Tavistock was opened on 22nd June, 1859, the train service consisted of five trains each way on weekdays and four trains on Sundays. All trains conveyed first, second and third class passengers, and the time taken in each direction between Plymouth and Tavistock was 50 minutes, with intermediate stops at Bickleigh and Horrabridge.

With the extension of the line to Launceston on 1st July, 1865, five trains ran through from Plymouth, but only four in the reverse direction, with two trains throughout on Sundays.

From the first the Launceston company was dissatisfied with the train timing, and made many applications to the South Devon Railway for improved services. A falling off in passengers during the half-year ended 30th June, 1868, due to an increase in fares in the previous year which failed to improve the revenue, led to a deputation meeting the South Devon company, when the question of times of trains and of fares was fully discussed. The intricacies of arranging suitable paths for trains on a single line were fully explained, and some improvements were promised. Fares were later restored to their former level, and this, with the natural growth of traffic, improved the position so far as numbers conveyed were concerned.

By 1872, however, the position regarding the train service had worsened with only three trains daily to Launceston, while 'the insignificant town of Tavistock' had five. By 1875 the service had increased to five trains each way daily, and two trains each way on Sundays.

The first up train from Launceston and Tavistock arrived at Plymouth at 9.42 am, and the first down train from Plymouth arrived at Launceston at 10.3 am. There was no train from Plymouth between 5 pm and 8 pm. The service was most inconvenient for business and professional people, and evoked much criticism.

The goods service consisted of a 12.40 am train from Plymouth to Launceston (Sundays included), and a return service from Launceston at 6.15 pm (Sundays excepted). The weekday line occupation commenced at Marsh Mills at 1.10 am with the 12.40 am goods from Plymouth, due Launceston at 5.30 am and ended at Launceston at 9.43 pm and at Marsh Mills at 9.9 pm (after the passing of the 7.35 pm train from Launceston).

Special instructions for working the goods traffic between Plymouth and Launceston, issued by the South Devon Company were:

The total number of trucks allowed on any one goods train between Tavistock and Plymouth was 28.

Up Trains.   TAVISTOCK AND LAUNCESTON BRANCH.   Week Days.

		1		2			3		4		5		6		7		8		9		10	
Distance	STATIONS.	B.G. Goods.		N.G. Goods These Trains will not run on Mondays.			N.G. Goods Conditional.		N.G. Passenger.		B.G. ssenger.		N.G. Passenger.		B.G. Passenger.		N.G. Passenger.		N.G. Passenger.		B.G. Passenger.	
		arr	dep	arr	dep	arr	dep	arr	dep	arr	dep	arr	dep	arr	dep	arr	dep	arr	dep	arr	dep	arr	dep
		a.m.	a.m.	a.m.	a.m.	a.m.	a.m	a m.	a.m.	a.m.	a.m.	a.m.	a m	a.m.	a.m.	a.m.	a.m.	p.m.	p.m.	p.m.	p.m.		
—	Devonport (s. w.)	...	...	...	3 0	...	4 0	...	7 40	...	...	10 20	...	...	...	11 43	...	1 50	...	...		
—	Plymouth (G.W.)	...	1 10	...	...	...	...	...	...	...	8 15	...	...	11 20	...	...	...	...	...	2 20		
¾	North Road	1 14	3 6	3 15	4 6	4 15	7 44	7 45	8 18	8 19	10 24	10 25	11 23	11 25	11 47	11 48	1 54	1 55	2 23	2 25		
1	Mutley ...	1 16		3 17		4 17	7 46	7 47	8 20	8 21	...	10 27	11 26	11 27	...	11 50	1 56	1 57	2 26	2 27		
2¾	Laira June	1 25	1 40	3 21	3 26	4 21	7 50		8 24		10 30		11 30		11 54		1 59		2 30			
4	Marsh Mills	1 50	X2 5	3 30	3 31	4 25	4 26	...	7 53	8 27	8 28	A	11 34	11 35	...	X11 56	...	X2 2	2 35	2 36		
7¾	Bickleigh ...	2 25	2 30	3 45	3 46	4 44	4 45	...	X8 4	8 38	X8 40	10 40	11 45	11X47	...	12 6	...	X2 12	2 45	2 47		
11	Yelverton	2 50	2 51	4 5	4 6	5 5	X5 10	8 13c		8 51	8 52	...	10X48	11 57	11 58	12 15c		c2 21	2 59	3 0		
12¾	Horrabridge	3 0	3 10	4 13	4 18	5 16	5 21	...	X8 18	8 57	X3 59	...	10 53	12 4	12 6	...	12 20	...	2 26	3 5	X3 7		
16½	Tavistock...	3 25	X4 10	4 33	X4 43	5 32	5 47	...	8 27	9 9	9 11	...	11 2	12 16	12 18	...	12 29	...	2 35	3 17	3 19		
20	Mary Tavy	4 22	4 27	4 55	4 56	5 59	6 0	8 35	X8 36	9 19	9 20	...	11X10	12 25	12 27	...	12 37	2 42	X2 44	3 27	3 28		
23	Lidford ...	4 42	5 15	5 10	...	6 12X	...	8 43	...	9 29	9 30	11 17	...	12 36	12 37	12 45X	...	2 52	...	3 37	3 38		
27½	Coryton ...	c. n.		...		...	...	...	...	9 41	9 42	...	...	12 48	12 49	...	...	...	...	3 49	3 50		
30¾	Lifton ...	5 35	6 5	...		...	...	...	...	9 49	9 50	...	...	12 56	12 57	...	...	...	...	3 57	3 58		
35½	Launceston	6 20	...	...		...	...	...	...	10 2	...	...	...	1 10	...	...	...	...	...	4 10	...		

A Stop by Signal to take up Passengers for Stations east of Lidford.   C Slacken for Train Staff.   For Crossing arrangements see pages (18 & 19).
No. 3 Train.—When it is required to run this Train, Mr. GALE will advise all Stations concerned,

Working timetable for September 1883.   *John M. Strange Collection*

Up Trains.   TAVISTOCK AND LAUNCESTON BRANCH.   Week Days,

		11		12		13		14		15		16		17		18		19	
Distance	STATIONS.	N.G. Passenger.		N.G. Goods.		N.G. Passenger.		B.G. Passenger.		N.G. Goods. from Friary.		N.G. Passenger.		B.G Passenger.		N.G. Goods from Friary.		B.G. Goods.	
		arr	dep	arr	dep	arr	dep	arr	dep	arr	dep	arr	dep	arr	dep	arr	dep	arr	dep
		p.m.	p.m.	p.m.	p.m.	p.m.	p.m.	p.m.	p.m.	p.m.	p.m.	p.m.	p.m.	p.m.	p.m.	p.m	p.m.	p.m.	p.m.
—	Devonport (s. w)	...	2 55	...	3 35	...	4 35	...	...		...	...	7 0	...	...		...	...	...
—	Plymouth (G.W)	...	...	...	...	...	...	...	5 35	For Friary Branch see page 60.	...	...	...	...	8 0	For Friary Branch see page 60.	...	...	11 10
¾	North Road	2 59	3 0	3 41	3 46	4 39	4 40	5 38	5 39		...	7 4	7 5	8 3	8 4		...	11 14	...
1	Mutley	3 1	3 2		3 48	...	4 43	5 40	5 41		...	...	7 7	8 5	8 6		...	11 16	...
2¾	Laira Junction...	3 5			3 53		4 46		5 44	5 50	6 5	7 10		8 9		11 10		11 20	11 35
4	Marsh Mills ...	3 8	3 13	3 58	X4 5	4 50	X4 58	5 47	5 50	6 10	X6 11	...	X7 13	8 12	8 13	11 15	X11 40	11 40X	11 55
7¾	Bickleigh	3 23	X3 24	4 19	4 22	...	5 7	5 58	X6 0	6 25	6 26	...	7 23	8 23	X8 25	11 55	11 56	12 15	12 20
11	Yelverton ...		3 34c	4 37	X4 44	c5 15		6 11	6 12	6 37	6 38	7 31c		8 37	X8 38	12 8	12 9	12 40	12 42
12¾	Horrabridge ...	3 38	4 39	4 51	4 55	...	5 20	6 17	6 19	6 43	X6 44	...	7 36	8 42	8 44	12 16	12 31	12 50	1 5
16½	Tavistock	3 47	3 48	5 7•	X5 42	...	•5 28	6 29	X6 31	6 56	7 12	...	7 44	8 54	X8 56	12 43	X1 2	1 20	sX2 20
20	Mary Tavy ...		3 55c	5 51	5 53	5 35	X5 36	6 39	6 40	7 21C		7 52	X7 54	9 4	X9 5	1 13	1 14	2 32	2 40
23	Lidford	4 2	...		6 4	...	5 43	...	6 49	6 50	7 29	...	8 2X	...	9 14	9 15	1 28	...	3 0	...
27½	Coryton ...	...	...	...	...	...	...	7 1	7 2	...	...	...	...	9 26	9 27	...	...	...	...
30¾	Lifton	...	...	...	...	...	...	7 9	X7 10	...	...	...	...	9 34	9 35	...	...	...	...
35½	Launceston ...	...	...	...	...	...	...	7 22	...	...	...	...	...	9 47	...	...	...	...	...

C Slacken for Train Staff.   S This Train will run above Tavistock only when required.   For Crossing arrangements see pages (18 & 19.)

Down Trains. TAVISTOCK AND LAUNCESTON BRANCH. Week Days.

Distance	STATIONS	1 N.G. Goods.			2 N.G. Conditional Goods.			3 B.G. Goods.			4 N.G. Goods Exeter to Friary.			5 N.G. Goods. A		
		arr	pass	dep	arr	pass	dep	arr	pass	dep	arr	pass	dep	arr	pass	dep
											a.m.		a.m.	a.m.		a.m.
—	Launceston	This Train will not run on Mondays.			...		...	This Train will not run on Mondays.			...		...	...		...
4¾	Lifton ...	a.m.		a.m.	...		...	a.m.		a.m.	...		...	...		...
8	Coryton ...	...		...	...		...	...		...	...		...	...		...
12½	Lidford ...	...		12 40	...		a.m. X1 30	...		3 35	7 0		7 2	7 25		7 35
15½	Mary Tavy	12 49		12 50	1 37		1 38	3 44		3 54	...		7 11	...		7 44
19	Tavistock ...	1 0X		X1 20	1 48		X2 0	4 5		4XX40	...		7 20	7 53		8 3
23	Horrabridge	1 32		1 37	2 12		2 13	4 53		5 3		7 32		8 15		X8 19
24½	Yelverton...	1 44		1 45	2 20		2 21	5 9		5 10		7 37		...		8 24
27¾	Bickleigh ..	1 54		1 55	2 30X		2 31	5 21		5 31	7 48		X8 5	8 35		X8 40
31½	Marsh Mills	2 4		X2 5	2 41		2 42	5 41		5 51	8 15		8 16	8 53		8 54
32¾	Laira... ...		2 9			2 46		5 56		6 6		8 19		8 58		A9 10
34½	Mutley ...		2 12			2 50			6 12		...		...		9 14	
34¾	North Road	2 14		2 19	2 52		2 59		6 14		...		...	9 15		9 16
35½	Plymouth (G.W.)	...		...	...		...	6 25		...	...		...	...		...
—	Devonport (S.W.)	2 25		...	3 5		...	...		...	...		...	9 22		...

Distance	STATIONS	6 B.G. Passenger.			7 N.G. Passenger.			8 B.G. Passenger.			9 N.G. Goods to Friary.			10 N.G. Passenger.		
		arr	pass	dep	arr	pass	dep	arr.	pass	dep	arr	pass	dep	arr	pass	dep
		a.m.		a.m.	a.m.		a.m.	a.m.		a.m.	p.m.		p.m.	p.m.		p.m.
—	Launceston	...		7 55	...		...	...		10 30	...		...	...		...
4¾	Lifton ...	8 3		8 4	...		...	10 38		10 39	...		...	...		...
8	Coryton ...	8 11		8 13	...		...	10 47		10 49	...		...	...		...
12½	Lidford ...	8 25		8 26	...		10 15	11 1		11 2	...		X12 47	1 13		1 14
15½	Mary Tavy	8 34		X8 35	...		10 23	11 10		X11 11	12 57		12 59		c1 20	
19	Tavistock ...	8 43		8 45	...		10 32	11 18		11 20	1 10		•1 36	...		•1 27
23	Horrabridge	8 57		X8 58	...		10 43	11 29		11 31	1 48		1 53	...		1 35
24½	Yelverton...	...		9 3	10 47		X10 48	11 35		11 36	...		1 58		c1 39	
27¾	Bickleigh ..	9 11		9 12	...		10 58	11 44		X11 46	2 8		X2 13		c1 46	
31½	Marsh Mills	9 20		9 21	...		11 8	11 54		X11 56	2 25		2 26	...		X1 54
32¾	Laira... ...		9 23			11 11			11 58			2 29			1 56	
34½	Mutley ...	9 26		9 28	...		11 15	12 3		12 4	For Friary Branch see pag 66.		...	...		2 0
34¾	North Road	9 29		9 30	11 16		11 18	12 5		12 6			...	2 1		2 3
35½	Plymouth (G.W.)	9 35		...	...		..	12 15		...			...	...		...
—	Devonport (S.W.)	...		...	11 23		...	...		...			...	2 8		...

A This Train will be divided at Laira Junction, the front part running to Friary (for Friary Branch, see page 60), and Crossings page (18 & 19). C Slacken for Train Staff.

No. 2 Train.—When it is required to run this Train, Mr. Gale will advise all stations concerned.

Working timetable for September 1883. *John M. Strange Collection*

Down Trains. TAVISTOCK AND LAUNCESTON BRANCH. Week Days.

Distance.	STATIONS.	11 B.G. Passenger.			12 N.G. Passenger.			13 N.G. Passenger.			14 N.G Passenger			15 B.G. Passenger		
		arr	pass	dep	arr	pass	dep	arr	pass	dep	arr	pass	dep	arr	pass	dep
		p.m.		p.m.	p.m.		p.m	p.m.		p.m.	p m.		p.m.	p.m.		p m
—	Launceston	...		2 5	...		...	...		...	...		...	...		5 40
4¾	Lifton ...	2 13		2 14	...		...	...		...	...		...	5 48		5 49
8	Coryton ...	2 22		2 24	...		...	...		...	...		...	5 56		5 58
12½	Lidford ...	2 35		2 36	3 7		3 8	4 19		4 20	5 16		5 18	6 10		6 11
15½	Mary Tavy	2 43		X2 44		3 13			c4 25		5 26		X5 35	6 19		6 20
19	Tavistock...	2 51		2 55	3 19X		3 26	4 31		4 32	...		X5 42	6 29		X6 31
23	Horrabridge	3 6		X3 8	3 36		X3 39		c4 40		...		5 50	6 41		X6 43
24½	Yelverton	3 14		3 15		3 43c		...		X4 44		5 54c		6 49		6 50
27¾	Bickleigh ...	3 24		X3 25	...		3 53		c4 50		6 0		X6 1	6 58		7 0
31½	Marsh Mills	3 35		3 37	...		X4 4	4 58		X5 0	6 9		X6 11	7 10		X7 12
32¾	Laira ...		3 39			4 6			5 2			6 13			7 14	
34½	Mutley ...	3 42		3 44	...		4 9	...		5 5	...		6 16	7 17		7 19
34¾	North Road	3 45		3 46	4 11		4 13	5 6		5 8	6 17		6 19	7 20		7 21
35½	Plymouth (G.W.)	3 51		...	...		...	...		...	...		...	7 26		...
	Devonport (S.W.)	...		...	4 17		...	5 13		...	6 24		...	...		...

Distance.	STATIONS.	16 N.G. Passenger.			17 N.G Passenger.			18 B.G. Passenger.			19 B.G. Goods.			20 N.G. Passenger.		
		arr.	pass	dep	arr	pass	dep	arr	pass	dep	arr	pass	dep	arr	pass	dep
		p.m.		p.m.	p.m.		p.m.	p.m.		p.m.	p.m.		p.m.	a.m.		p.m.
—	Launceston	...		...	...		...	...		8 5	...		6 30	...		...
4¾	Lifton ...	...		...	...		..	8 13		8 14	6 45		X7 10	...		...
8	Coryton ...	...		...	...		...	8 21		8 23		C R		...		...
12½	Lidford ...	7 43		7 47	8 9		•8 10	8 35		•8 36	8 0X		••8 46	10 53		10 54
15½	Mary Tavy	...		X7 54		8 17c		8 44		8 45	8 56		X 9 10		11 1c	
19	Tavistock...	...		8 1	...		8 24	8 54		X8 56	9 22		9 58	...		11 9
23	Horrabridge		c 8 9		8 32		8 33	9 6		9 8	10 11		10 20	...		11 18
24½	Yelverton		c 8 16		8 38		X8 39	9 14		9 15	10 28		10 29		11 22c	
27¾	Bickleigh ...	8 23		X8 25	8 47		8 51	9 23		9 25	10 38		10 46		11 29c	
31½	Marsh Mills	...		8 33	8 59		9 1	9 35		9 37	10 57		11 5	11 37X		X11 39
32¾	Laira ...		8 35			9 4			9 39			C R			11 41	
34½	Mutley ...	...		8 38	...		9 7	9 42		9 44		11 17		...		11 45
34¾	North Road	8 39		8 40	9 8		9 10	9 43		9 46		11 18		11 46		11 48
35½	Plymouth (G.W.)	...		...	...		...	9 51		...	11 20		...	...		...
	Devonport (S.W.)	8 45		...	9 15		...	...		...	...		...	11 53		...

C Slacken for Train Staff. For Crossing arrangements see page (18 & 19).

Two views from early this century of Coryton looking towards Plymouth. The track layout at that time consisted of a single siding, which was linked to the running line by means of a 'scissors' crossover. The single passenger platform had a length of 300 ft. *(Both) Lens of Sutton*

All goods trains had to stop dead on the up journey at Marsh Mills to apply hand brakes as required and the speed of goods trains was not to exceed 20 mph.

Most of the goods work was performed at Tavistock during the night turn of duty between 1 am and 5 am but there is no evidence that the noise of shunting during this period disturbed the inhabitants of the town.

On 17th May, 1876, South Western trains commenced running over the mixed gauge between Lydford, Tavistock, Marsh Mills, Plymouth and Devonport. Lydford then became the busiest station on the line, and by 1878 was dealing with the following:

		Weekdays		Sundays	
		Passenger	Goods	Passenger	Goods
Up Trains	South Devon	5	2	2	1
	South Western	7	4	1	2
Down Trains	South Devon	5	2	2	1
	South Western	7	4	1	1

The line was open continuously and as both broad and narrow gauge trains were involved, the working was intense and complicated. Crossing of trains took place at Marsh Mills, Yelverton, Horrabridge, Tavistock, Mary Tavy, and Lydford.

At Tavistock, 16 up and 16 down trains were dealt with daily. This heavy occupation of a single line, coupled with the preference given to South Devon trains, created difficulties in bad weather and caused late running and frequent delays, but despite the obvious operating difficulties in such circumstances there was no serious accident involving the death of a passenger.

Passenger traffic continued to grow, and the train service to Tavistock increased with it. By 1906 there were eleven trains daily between Plymouth Millbay and Tavistock, with two additional workings on Wednesdays and Saturdays; and five, (six on Fridays and Saturdays), continuing to Launceston.

After World War I, an augmented service catered for a traffic which made the railway to Tavistock one of the busiest branch lines in the west country. Traffic to the Moor developed rapidly with the introduction of half-day and evening cheap tickets from Plymouth, and on Wednesdays, Saturdays, Sundays, and on Bank Holidays during the summer period, special trains were run.

In the winter large numbers of people travelled to Plymouth on Saturdays for shopping, football or entertainment, and the last train from Plymouth at 11.10 pm frequently carried up to 200 passengers.

During World War II a reduced train service dealt with much additional traffic as a result of people moving out of Plymouth to be away from a vulnerable area. After the war the passenger traffic maintained a good level until 1950, when the abolition of petrol rationing, the extension of Plymouth's bus services, and the growth of private motoring, caused a large decrease in the number of rail passengers.

By 1959 there were 8 trains to Tavistock daily from Plymouth North Road, with 10 on Saturdays, and 3 trains to Launceston daily and 2 additional on Saturdays (three Sunday trains were withdrawn in 1958), and this service operated until 31st December, 1962 when the line was closed.

Table 95 **PLYMOUTH, PRINCETOWN, TAVISTOCK SOUTH and LAUNCESTON**

Miles	Week Days only	am ②	am	am ②		am E	am S		pm	pm Y		pm W	pm S	pm		pm ②		pm		pm D	pm S		
—	**Plymouth** (North Rd.) dep	5 50	7 10	7 45	..	1040	10 40	..	12 8	1242	..	1 48	2 10	3 5	..	5 25	..	6 23	..	8 24	8 24	..	..
3	Marsh Mills	5 57	7 18	7 52	..	1047	10 47	..	1215	1249	..	1 55	2 17	3 12	..	5 32	..	6 30	..	8 31	8 31	..	..
4¼	Plym Bridge Platform	..	..	..	..	1051	10 51	..	1220	1253	..	1 59	2 21	3 16	..	5 36	..	..	..	..	..	..	..
7	Bickleigh	6 7	7 29	8 1	..	1058	10 58	..	1228	1 0	..	2 7	2 28	3 26	..	5 43	..	6 40	..	8 41	8 41	..	..
7¾	Shaugh Bridge Platform	..	7 33	8 5	..	11 3	11 3	..	1234	1 5	..	2 12	2 34	3 31	..	5 48	..	6 44	..	8 45	8 45	..	..
9	Clearbrook Halt	..	7 37	8 10	..	11 8	11 8	..	1240	1 10	..	2 17	2 39	3 36	..	5 53	..	6 49	..	8 49	8 49	..	..
10¼	Yelverton arr	6 17	7 42	8 15	..	1114	11 14	..	1246	1 14	..	2 22	2 43	3 41	..	5 58	..	6 54	..	8 54	8 54	..	..
—	Yelverton dep	☞ RAIL SERVICE WITHDRAWN. A road service is operated between Yelverton, Dousland and Princetown and Tavistock and Princetown by the Western National Omnibus Company.															..	..	..	..	..	..	..
12	Dousland																..	..	..	..	..	..	..
13¼	Burrator Halt																..	..	..	..	..	..	..
16½	Ingra Tor Halt																..	..	..	..	..	..	..
19¼	King Tor Halt																..	..	..	..	..	..	..
20¾	**Princetown** arr																..	..	..	..	..	..	..
—	Yelverton dep	6 18	7 43	8 16	..	1116	11 16	..	1249	1 15	..	2 24	2 44	3 42	..	5 59	..	6 55	..	8 55	8 55	..	..
11¾	Horrabridge	6 21	7 46	8 20	..	1120	11 20	..	1252	1 18	..	2 28	2 48	3 46	..	6 2	..	6 58	..	8 58	8 58	..	..
14¾	Whitchurch Down P'form	6 27	7 51	8 25	..	1125	11 25	..	1257	1 24	..	2 33	2 52	3 51	..	6 7	..	7 3	..	9 3	9 3	..	..
15¾	Tavistock South **A**	6 30	8U 0	8 28	..	1128	11Z35	..	1U 6	1 27	..	2 36	2 56	4K 0	..	6 11	..	7U11	..	9 6	9T14	..	..
19	Mary Tavy & Blackdown Hlt	..	8 6	..	..	②	11 41	..	1 15	②	..	②	②	4 6	..	..	..	7 20	..	②	9 20	..	..
22¼	Lydford	..	8 14	..	..	..	11 49	..	1 24	..	..	..	..	4 13	..	..	..	7 28	..	..	9 27	..	..
25¼	Liddaton Halt	..	8 21	..	..	..	11 55	..	1 30	..	..	..	..	4 20	..	..	..	7 35	..	..	9 34	..	..
26¾	Coryton	..	8 25	..	..	..	12 0	..	1 35	..	..	..	..	4 24	..	..	..	7 40	..	..	9 38	..	..
30	Lifton	..	8 33	..	..	..	12 6	..	1 43	..	..	..	..	4 31	..	..	..	7 47	..	..	9 45	..	..
34¾	**Launceston** arr	..	8 45	..	..	..	12 15	..	1 52	..	..	..	..	4 40	..	..	..	7 55	..	..	9 55	..	..

Miles	Week Days only	am ②	am	am ②		am		pm ②	pm S		pm		pm ②		pm		pm ②		pm D ②		pm S		
—	**Launceston** dep	..	7 5	..	..	10 15	..	..	1250	..	2 5	..	..	..	5 40	..	..	..	..	..	8 25	..	..
4¾	Lifton	..	7 16	..	..	10 23	..	..	1258	..	2 13	..	..	..	5 48	..	..	..	..	..	8 33	..	..
8	Coryton	..	7 24	..	..	10 30	..	..	1 4	..	2 20	..	..	..	5 55	..	..	..	..	..	8 39	..	..
9½	Liddaton Halt	..	7 29	..	..	10 36	..	..	1 10	..	2 27	..	..	..	6 2	..	..	..	..	..	8 44	..	..
12½	Lydford	..	7 42	..	..	10 46	..	..	1G23	..	2 40	..	..	..	6 17	..	..	..	..	..	8 55	..	..
15¾	Mary Tavy & Blackdown Hlt	..	7 49	..	..	10 52	..	..	1 28	..	2 46	..	..	..	6 23	..	..	..	..	..	9 0	..	..
19	Tavistock South **A**	6 47	8U 0	8 45	..	11U 2	..	1233	1U39	..	3K 0	..	4 30	..	6U35	..	7 10	..	9 25	..	9Y25	..	..
20	Whitchurch Down P'form	6 50	8 3	8 48	..	11 5	..	1235	1 42	..	3 3	..	4 33	..	6 39	..	7 13	..	9 28	..	9 28	..	..
23	Horrabridge	6 57	8 10	8 54	..	11 12	..	1243	1 48	..	3 10	..	4 40	..	6 47	..	7 20	..	9 35	..	9 35	..	..
24½	Yelverton arr	7 1	8 15	9 1	..	11 16	..	1247	1 53	..	3 15	..	4 45	..	6 52	..	7 25	..	9 39	..	9 39	..	..
—	Mls. **Princetown** dep	☞ RAIL SERVICE WITHDRAWN. A road service is operated between Yelverton, Dousland and Princetown and Tavistock and Princetown by the Western National Omnibus Company.															..	..	..	..	..	..	..
—	1½ King Tor Halt																..	..	..	..	..	..	..
—	4½ Ingra Tor Halt																..	..	..	..	..	..	..
—	7½ Burrator Halt																..	..	..	..	..	..	..
—	8¾ Dousland																..	..	..	..	..	..	..
—	10½ Yelverton arr																..	..	..	..	..	..	..
—	Yelverton dep	7 2	8 16	9 2	..	11 18	..	1248	1 54	..	3 16	..	4 46	..	6 55	..	7 26	..	9 40	..	9 40	..	..
25¾	Clearbrook Halt	7 5	8 19	9 5	..	11 21	..	1252	1 57	..	3 19	..	4 49	..	6 59	..	7 29	..	9 42	..	9 42	..	..
27	Shaugh Bridge Platform	7 8	8 22	9 8	..	11 24	..	1255	2 0	..	3 22	..	4 52	..	7 2	..	7 32	..	9 45	..	9 45	..	..
27¾	Bickleigh	7 11	8 26	9 11	..	11 28	..	1 1	2 4	..	3 25	..	4 57	..	7 6	..	7 35	..	9 48	..	9 48	..	..
30½	Plym Bridge Platform	..	8 31	..	..	11 33	..	1 6	2 9	..	..	..	5 2	..	7 11	..	..	..	..	..	..	..	..
31¾	Marsh Mills	7 19	8 35	9 19	..	11 38	..	1 10	2 13	..	3 34	..	5 8	..	7 16	..	7 42	..	9 56	..	9 56	..	..
34¾	**Plymouth** (North Rd.) arr	7 28	8 47	9 26	..	11 47	..	1 20	2 20	..	3 45	..	5 17	..	7 25	..	7 50	..	10 5	..	10 5	..	..

A 1 mile to Tavistock North Station
D Except Saturdays. Commences 29th April, 1957
E Except Saturdays
G Arr 3 minutes *earlier*
K Arr 6 minutes *earlier*
S Saturdays only
T Arr 9 6 pm
U Arr 4 minutes *earlier*
V Arr 9 8 pm
W Except Saturdays. Through from Saltash (Table 94)
Y Saturdays only. Through Train Saltash (Table 94)
Z Arr 7 minutes *earlier*
② Second class only

Timetable for September 1956.

Up to 1914 the goods traffic was dealt with by a night service of freight trains. These were: 12.15 am Laira to Tavistock, extended to Lydford as required, and returning to Laira; 8 pm Launceston to Laira; 1.45 am Laira to Launceston. The shunting at stations was carried out by the guard of the train and a brakesman, a grade later replaced by that of shunter.

When the night working ceased, the freight service consisted of separate trains from Laira to Launceston, to Tavistock and to Horrabridge, and return, with a daily service from Tavistock to Pitt's Cleave Quarry sidings.

Some Notes on Signalling

The signalling provided on the Tavistock line during its earliest days was rudimentary by the standards of a later period. Broad gauge-type 'disc and crossbar' signals were installed at stations and other places, and these consisted of large circular discs mounted on top of a post, with a crossbar attached at right angles beneath it; when the disc faced oncoming trains the signal meant 'all right', whereas if the signal was rotated so that the crossbar faced oncoming trains the signal indicated 'danger'.

The line was re-signalled in connection with the introduction of London & South Western services between Lydford and Plymouth in 1876, the well-known signalling firm of Saxby & Farmer being engaged to carry out this work. Interlocked track and signalling layouts were provided in connection with this major resignalling scheme, while the original disc and crossbar signals were largely replaced by conventional semaphore signals. At the same time, standard Saxby & Farmer type signal boxes (which could be easily distinguished by the provision of small upper lights above the main windows) appeared at many of the intermediate stations.

The interlocking apparatus was brought into use on the line as follows: Marsh Mills, 20th March, 1876; Bickleigh, 21st February, 1876; Horrabridge, 25th October, 1875; Tavistock, 1st March, 1876; Mary Tavy, 2nd November, 1875; Lydford, 26th October, 1875.

Train staff and ticket operation - which was never adopted on the single line portions of the South Devon main line - was introduced between Lydford and Marsh Mills in May 1876. This mode of operation enabled two or more trains to follow each other in the same direction along the single line, the actual train staff being carried on the last train in an up or down series.

To prevent confusion, distinctive train staffs and tickets were employed for use in each section, the various shapes and colours being as shown below:

Section	Form of staff/ticket	Colour of ticket
Marsh Mills & Bickleigh	Half-round	Brown
Bickleigh & Yelverton	Oblong	Blue
Yelverton & Horrabridge	Six-sided	White
Horrabridge & Tavistock	Tri-angular	Green
Tavistock & Mary Tavy	Square	Pink
Mary Tavy & Lydford	Round	Yellow

The interior of the third signal box at Bickleigh c. 1958.

The first box, a standard Saxby & Farmer design, was situated on the up platform but the Board of Trade's Inspecting Officer refused permission for the box to be used. The down facing points were 240 yards from the box and the up facing points 170 yards from the box, far in excess of the maximum 120 yards permitted. This signal box was converted into a goods shed by having its operating floor and staircase removed and sliding doors fixed to the front of it. As the goods shed it remained in use until the station's closure.

As a result of the Board of Trade's decision a second box was built at the Plymouth end of the crossing loop and a ground frame, bolt locked from the signal box, was situated at the Yelverton end of the crossing loop to work the adjacent facing points. This box opened on 21st February, 1876 as part of the resignalling works to allow the 'narrow gauge' LSWR trains to commence running over the previous broad gauge-only lines of the South Devon Railway in May 1876. The box contained a 14-lever Saxby & Farmer frame. The LSWR opened its independent route between Lidford and Plymouth in 1890 and gave up their option of running powers over the Tavistock and Launceston branch. As a result the GWR, which had taken over the operation of the line from the South Devon Railway in 1876, altered the direction of running. Up trains became down trains and down trains became up trains.

In 1912 it was decided to open a new (third) signal box because by this time the maximum distance facing points could be worked from a box had been increased to 250 yards. The box was situated on the up (previously down) platform opposite the shell of the first box. The box contained a 23-lever stud frame.

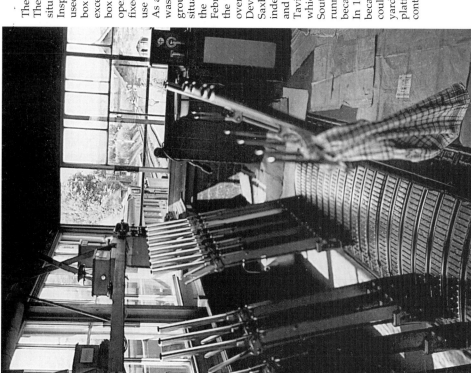

Adrian Vaughan Collection

The train staff & ticket system had a relatively short life on the Launceston branch, and by 1895 the branch had been equipped with the electric train staff. Electric train token apparatus was subsequently employed between Lifton and Launceston. By 1948, the sections were as follows:

Marsh Mills & Bickleigh	Electric train staff
Bickleigh & Yelverton	Electric train staff
Yelverton & Horrabridge	Electric train staff
Horrabridge & Tavistock	Electric train staff
Tavistock & Lydford	Electric train staff
Lydford & Lifton	Electric train staff
Lifton & Launceston	Electric train token

In 1957 the signal box at Yelverton was taken out of use, and the electric token system was introduced on an extended section between Bickleigh and Horrabridge.

The motor trolley system of permanent way maintenance was introduced between Marsh Mills and Horrabridge on 28th February, 1933, and from Horrabridge to Launceston on 6th March, 1933. Permanent Way Staff consisted of three gangs, situated at Yelverton, Tavistock and Lifton.

Speed restrictions at the time of closure were as follows: between Tavistock Junction and Lydford, 40 mph; Lydford to Coryton, 35 mph; Coryton to Lifton, 40 mph; Lifton to Launceston, 45 mph.

Before leaving the subject of signalling it is interesting to note that, in South Devon days some of the intermediate sidings on the branch were equipped with an unusual type of signal. These consisted of detonators fixed to an iron rod which was, in turn, attached to the base of the signals protecting the siding; (i.e. an early form of detonator placer machine). Should drivers run over the detonators they had to stop their trains as speedily as possible. The signals were placed at the following sidings: Lifton (Cawdron) Quarry, Leat Mill, Brentor, Yelverton and Shaugh.

Some Motive Power Notes

After the abandonment of the atmospheric system on the South Devon Railway in 1848 the locomotive power was supplied by the Great Western company. The locomotives sent were of the latter company's standard classes, of which the 'Leo' class of 2-4-0s with 5 ft 0 in. coupled wheels and 15 in. x 18 in. cylinders was the most numerous, but none was really suitable. All the GWR engines had returned eastward long before the railway had reached Tavistock.

Two 4-4-0 saddle tanks, *Corsair* and *Brigand*, built at Swindon in 1849 for working on the South Devon, set the pattern for all succeeding passenger engines supplied to that company. They had 6 ft 0 in. coupled wheels, 3 ft 6 in. bogie wheels and 17 in. x 24 in. cylinders.

Between 1851 and 1866 (when the company took control) locomotives for the SDR were supplied under contract. They were all saddle tanks of Gooch design, the passenger engines being very similar to *Corsair* and *Brigand*. The first batch,

An interesting broadside view of the South Devon Railway 0-6-0ST goods locomotive *Dragon* (later GWR No. 2164), probably photographed outside Launceston engine shed. This broad gauge engine was built by Avonside Engine Co. in 1872.   *P.J.T. Reed Collection*

An unidentified locomotive arrives with a passenger train for Plymouth at Coryton *c.* 1906.
                                                                                                L&GRP

twelve 4-4-0ST engines delivered between October 1851 and April 1853, had 5 ft 9 in. coupled wheels and 17 in. x 24 in. cylinders and were withdrawn between 1873 and 1884.

Another twelve 4-4-0STs, which had 5 ft 6 in. coupled wheels and 16½ in. x 24 in. cylinders, came in 1859-60. All were built by Slaughter, Gruning & Co of Bristol, and had been ordered in anticipation of the opening of the Cornwall and Tavistock lines. Of these *Gazelle, Antelope, Wolf* and *Hector* came to Plymouth, and *Giraffe* to Tavistock. They cost £2,790 each when new; *Giraffe* was transferred to Launceston in 1865, where it was joined by *Castor*, the last of four later engines of the class (believed to have had 5 ft 9 in. coupled wheels at first) built between 1863 and 1865, during which time the title of the maker's was altered from Slaughter, Gruning & Co to the Avonside Engine Co.

During this same period (1851-66) only twelve goods engines were delivered - all 0-6-0 saddle tanks. Of these *Dido* with 4 ft 6 in. wheels and 16½ in. x 24 in. cylinders, and *Ajax* with 4 ft 9 in. wheels and 17 in. x 24 in. cylinders, both built in 1860, are known to have worked on the branch.

In 1872, *Bulkeley*, an 0-6-0 side tank with 4 ft 6 in. wheels and 17 in. x 24 in. cylinders, recently purchased from the GWR, also went to Launceston as did, after the GWR had taken over, some of the 'Hawthorn' class converted to saddle tanks. These were 2-4-0STs with 5 ft 0 in. coupled wheels and 17 in. x 24 in. cylinders and included *Melling* and *Ostrich*.

For many years *Giraffe* was in the charge of driver Joe Booth; *Castor* of Jameson Davis, and *Bulkeley* of Dan Ware.

In 1876 narrow gauge rails were added between Lydford and Keyham for the use of the LSWR until 1890, when an alternative route into Plymouth was made available. The Beyer, Peacock 'Metropolitan', (or 'Plymouth') 4-4-0 tanks, which were designed for the LSWR passenger service, proved unsatisfactory, being replaced by Beattie 2-4-0s, while during the 1880s Adams 4-4-2 tanks and '395' class 0-6-0s are among the classes known to have worked the line.

Returning to the GWR, various Dean passenger tanks of the '35XX' series were in evidence around the time of gauge conversion, while engines of the '3521' class, as altered to 4-4-0 tender engines between 1899 and 1902, persisted on the branch up to World War I. Nos. 3528/35/50/54/56 are known to have been shedded at Launceston.

Of the goods engines employed, the saddle tank No. 1897 regularly worked the Tavistock goods for many years. The last broad gauge engine to work on the Tavistock branch was *Heron* (GWR No. 2134), a 4-4-0 saddle tank which worked the 9.44 pm Plymouth to Tavistock on 20th May, 1892, returning with the empty stock to Plymouth and thence to Swindon.

'Duke' class 4-4-0s with small tenders were permitted to work on the branch, ramps being provided for the turntables at Tavistock and Launceston to allow tender engines to turn. *King Arthur*, at least, was stationed at Launceston in 1912-13.

In 1904 a prototype small-wheeled 2-6-2 tank locomotive was built by the Great Western, and this initial engine having proved satisfactory, ten further locomotives of the same type were ordered in 1905. These engines became the '31XX' (later '44XX') class, and they were to operate on the Launceston and

Princetown lines for many years.

The '44XX' class engines had 4 ft 1 in. coupled wheels and 16½ in. x 24 in. outside cylinders. They were numbered in the '31XX' series, the first members of the class to work on the line being Nos. 3101 and 3104. In 1912 the locomotives were re-numbered in the '44XX' series, and at one time or another all eleven members of the class appeared on the routes to Princetown or Launceston.

The visually-similar '45XX' class with 4 ft 7½ in. coupled wheels also worked for many years on the Launceston route, while their small-wheeled sisters of the '44XX' class remained hard at work on the heavily-graded Princetown branch until the 1950s.

In May 1932 *The Railway Magazine* reported that '44XX' 2-6-2T No. 4402, which was stationed at Plymouth (Laira) for work on the Princetown line, had been involved in a series of experiments in connection with the use of compressed air brakes instead of the standard GWR vacuum brakes. Another experiment conducted at this time involved the use of a flange oiling device which was supposed to reduce excessive wear of rails and flanges on sharp curves.

The first members of the '45XX' class were fitted with flat-topped side tanks resembling those on the '44XX' class, but from No. 4575 onwards the engines were fitted with larger, 1,300 gallon side tanks with sloping tops, Nos. 4575-4599 and 5500-5574 all having the sloping-topped tanks. Both variants of the '45XX' class appeared on the Launceston route, and with the '44XX' class, these distinctive small prairie tanks could justifiably be called the Launceston branch engines *par excellence*.

With the introduction of the '45XX' and '55XX' class 2-6-2Ts the line again became virtually a tank engine preserve. Engines of this class remained to the end; their load was 220 tons to Yelverton and 240 tons beyond.

Most of the GW larger classes were allowed but only to Yelverton, there being insufficient clearance beyond, and the engines being too heavy for Walkham Viaduct. The standard load for a 'Castle' was 350 tons; 'Star', 'Hall' and 'Grange' class 4-6-0s were allowed 285 tons, and 'Bulldog' 4-4-0s 220 tons.

Steam railmotors were introduced (to Tavistock) early in the century, and these were superseded by auto-train services. For several years, older small tank engines were fitted for auto working, some being painted to harmonise with the trailer cars. '517' class 0-4-2Ts, 'Metropolitan' class 2-4-0Ts, and 0-6-0 saddle (or pannier) tanks of the '2021' and '1076' classes were mainly involved. Nos. 2120 and 2140 were at Plymouth for several years - at first encased in dummy coachwork - while double-framed engines of the '1076' class were largely used.

In the 1930s new engines were built for auto working, and of these the '64XX' 0-6-0PTs with 4 ft 7½ in. wheels, and '14XX' 0-4-2Ts with 5 ft 2 in. coupled wheels, in particular, were used on the branch. In 1954-5 a few '57XX' class 0-6-0PTs of the '87XX', '36XX' and '37XX' series were occasionally used.

Accidents

During the history of the South Devon & Tavistock and the Launceston lines there were no reports of accidents involving the death of a passenger, although the operating conditions over a single line of mixed gauge with its intense occupation during the period 1876 to 1890 did not lend itself to smooth working. The following incidents are of interest:

On 18th April, 1869 the 9.20 am passenger train from Tavistock, after passing Magpie Viaduct, came to a sudden stop. The passengers heard a sound of something breaking and upon examination it was found that the engine pistons were broken. Another engine was telegraphed for and the train then proceeded having been delayed for only one hour.

Considering the lack of communication in those days and the fact that the guard or fireman had to walk to Horrabridge to advise the staff there of the incident, no time was lost in telegraphing for assistance, or in supplying another engine from Plymouth. Even by modern standards this would have been considered good working.

Another case concerned the 11 am train from Waterloo to Devonport on 18th November, 1885. The train was hauled by LSWR '395' class 0-6-0 No. 442, and the formation included two guards vans and a carriage truck (coach). After proceeding about a mile from Yelverton the train oscillated so considerably that passengers were aware that it was derailed. After going about one hundred yards the train, except for the engine tender and the first van, came to a stand. Passengers on the coach alighted and found that the front portion of the train had gone over an embankment and had overturned about seventy yards from the line.

The front guard found himself under his van but succeeded in getting free with only a cut on his hand. The fireman, John Wills of Exeter, was found lying twenty yards down the embankment, having been thrown clear, and seriously injured. The driver was found beneath his engine with a bar of iron across his face and his arm about a brake handle. He was dead. The front compartment of the coach next to the van was smashed but the two passengers who were in it escaped injury.

At the time of the accident the train was going at a steady rate of from twenty to twenty-five miles an hour according to passengers' statements. The cause of the accident was not apparent; the line was torn up over about 150 yards, but the carriages left on the line were not extensively damaged.

At the subsequent inquiry, a permanent way official who was on the train at the time said that the brake went on immediately after they had passed the 6¼ mile post and they came to a stop. The gradient at that point was 1 in 58 and the radius of the curve was 20 chains. Repairs on the line had not recently been necessary. The type of engine involved (0-6-0) ran very stiffly going around the curves and was unsteady down the inclines. Another permanent way official said the cant of the outer rail was about 7 inches, which was a good cant for a train going about forty miles an hour over that kind of curve. On the broad gauge line the cant was 11 inches. It was later recorded that the cause of the accident was a broken coupling.

Staff

In the early days of the railway, the traffic department staff usually consisted of the following grades:

Employee	Salary or wage rate
Station Master	£95 to £105 per annum
Booking Constable	20s. to 24s. 6d. per week
Watchman	16s. per week
Parcels Porters	
Goods Porters	12s. to 20s. per week
Station Porters	
Shunters	18s. per week
Passenger Guards	25s. per week
Goods Guards	24s. per week
Switchman	20s. per week

Bonus payments were made to most grades, and switchmen received a premium of £5.

In 1874 Tavistock and Launceston were the only stations on that section of the railway with station masters, booking constables being in charge of the less important stations. Tavistock also had a parcels porter, a goods porter, three porters and a shunter.

Launceston also had a parcels porter, four porters, a passenger guard and two goods guards. Horrabridge had a booking constable, a watchman, and two porters. Lifton had a booking constable and a watchman. Two switchmen were employed at Tavistock Junction.

All staff worked a twelve-hour day, and night duty was necessary at Tavistock, Lifton, Horrabridge and Launceston, these stations dealing with most of the goods traffic which was conveyed by night goods trains.

There were no agreements with trade unions in those days. The rates and conditions of service were fixed by the management. There was no difficulty in securing the staff required. Many sons followed in the steps of their fathers, service on the railway being continued in many cases through two or three generations. Railway employment was looked upon as something worth having; it provided security and offered promotion to those with ambition.

The local station master was a person of some importance in those days, and it was a good thing to secure his support to an application for employment. Recommendations from the local squire, the parson, school master or other well-known celebrity or person of standing, were eagerly sought.

Each applicant had to be interviewed, and if considered suitable, was given a medical test and had to show himself proficient in the 'three Rs'.

Once employed, there were annual increments of wages, usually a shilling per week, granted to certain grades upon a favourable report being submitted by the local station master or chief inspector. Promotion to higher grade was by merit, and suitability. A good standard of conduct was required, and penalties were inflicted. These took the form of fines, cautions or suspensions and dismissal for the more serious matters. Fines ranged from sixpence to half-a-crown, the latter being a stiff penalty.

Staff who became intoxicated when on duty, who were insolent, absent without leave or irregular in attendance, were often dismissed the service. Fines were imposed for the less serious charges which included carelessness in working causing minor derailments; neglect of duty to attend to passengers; failing to charge a passenger excess on his luggage; accepting a gratuity from a passenger; for being in a signal box without authority. It would seem that almost every misdemeanour was reported and that little was left to the discretion of the local station master.

Upon appointment, every railwayman had to sign an undertaking that he would abide by the rules and regulations laid down in the official Rule Book, commonly called 'The Railwayman's Bible'.

Some companies imposed very exacting conditions of employment, as the following extracts from an old Rule Book, issued in 1856, will prove:

> No instances of intoxication, singing, whistling, or levity while on duty will be overlooked.
> Every person to come on duty daily, clean in his person and clothes, shaved and his boots blacked.
> All persons, especially those in uniform, must keep their hair cut.
> Every person not on duty on Sundays or Holy Days, is requested to attend a place of worship, as it will be the means of promotion when vacancies occur. Persons having passes are to ride in the fourth wagon from the last in the train, and at all times in a sitting position upon the bottom of the wagon.

The total staff employed on the Launceston and Tavistock line in 1874 was 33. In 1903 the total was 67, an exceptionally high figure compared with the yearly figures for the next 30 years, when the average was 50.

A Launceston-Plymouth train *c*. 1955 seen between Tavistock and Laira Junctions behind '45XX' class 2-6-2T No. 5531. Note the 6-wheel Siphon immediately behind the engine.

M. Daly

A turn of the century view of the station approach at Millbay, showing the stone-built station buildings. This station was closed to passengers after the April 1941 air raids.   *Lens of Sutton*

A view along the platform towards the buffer stops at Millbay in 1913. Platform 2 is to the left, while platform 3 is on the right.   *L&GRP*

Chapter Seven

The Route Described
Plymouth to Tavistock

When first opened throughout to Plymouth in April 1849 the South Devon Railway had terminated near the docks at Millbay. Built of timber, the first Millbay station featured three platform lines beneath an overall roof, with an additional platform for fish traffic on the east side of the wooden train shed.

Plymouth Millbay

The original Millbay station was rebuilt at the end of the 19th century to provide a more modern terminus with substantial, stone station buildings in place of the earlier wooden facilities. There were, however, still three main terminal platforms with a shorter bay on the east side; these were numbered from 1 to 4, platform 1 being the bay while Nos. 2, 3 and 4 were the main terminal roads. In its rebuilt form the station lost its 'Brunelian' style overall roof, the four platforms being covered by commodious canopies.

In October 1895 it was proposed that £4,500 should be spent on a signalling scheme for the new Millbay station, and a 117-lever signal, box was eventually erected. The new cabin was inspected by the Board of Trade Inspector on 10th July, 1899 - at which time it contained 99 working levers, three spare levers and three spaces. As a result of a subsequent re-signalling, carried out in 1914, Millbay acquired a new 115-lever box.

Plymouth North Road

Although adequate in relation to local traffic, Plymouth Millbay was designed for use as a terminus, and trains continuing through from Paddington to Penzance (or vice versa) had to reverse. To eradicate this problem, a new station known as Plymouth North Road was constructed to the north of the original terminus, on a site that was more convenient for the growing population of Plymouth.

Built to plans drawn up by Peter J. Margary, North Road was opened in 1877. Like Plymouth Millbay, it was constructed of timber, and the platforms were covered by an overall roof structure with a span of 150 ft. The roof consisted of two double-pitched sections, each of which had a width of 46 ft. The centre part of the station was left uncovered to facilitate smoke emission, though the centre tracks were spanned by transverse girders that linked the two train sheds.

By the turn-of-the-century North Road station consisted of four through platforms beneath the overall roof, with additional, dead-end bays on each side; unusually, the northern and southernmost through lines were served by two platform faces - which gave travellers the option of alighting from either side of their trains!

Plymouth North Road was controlled from two signal boxes. These were

Collett '14XX' class 0-4-2T No. 1434 stands in the platforms at Plymouth Millbay on 12th July, 1955. The stock will be worked empty to North Road and then form the auto-train service to Tavistock. *R.C. Riley*

Between Millbay and Plymouth North Road was Belmont Sidings (*left*), seen here in August 1961. The carriage sidings on the right were known as Harwell Street Sidings. *R.C. Riley*

Plymouth North Road as seen from the station approach. This station was opened in 1877, and extensively rebuilt in the 1950s. *Lens of Sutton*

A general view of Plymouth North Road station around 1913, showing the 'double roof' structure with its uncovered centre position. *L&GRP*

Plymouth Mutley station viewed from the footbridge in 1921. The station had no goods facilities of any kind. *L&GRP*

Plymouth Mutley station seen from above the tunnel *c.* 1939; the station was barely half a mile from North Road. *Stephenson Locomotive Society*

designated Plymouth North Road East and Plymouth North Road West boxes, and both were sited on the north side of the main running lines; in 1908 North Road West box had a 59-lever frame while North Road East was equipped with a 48-lever frame.

The Great Western started to rebuild the station during the 1930s, the idea being that the existing four-platform station would be remodelled, with seven through platforms and extensive new buildings. This ambitious programme was halted by World War II, but in 1956 British Railways commenced a new, £1,800,000 modernisation scheme. The rebuilt station was officially opened on 26th March, 1962, and in its new form North Road consisted of seven through platforms with additional bays for parcels and local traffic. The buildings were entirely rebuilt in an uncompromisingly modern style, incorporating extensive glass and concrete platform coverings and a ten-storey office and administrative building housing the staffs of the District Superintendent, the District Engineer and various other departments. A new power signal box, at the western end of the rebuilt station, controlled the movements of all trains within an area bounded by Millbay and Keyham in the west and Laira in the east.

Launceston branch trains ran to and from Plymouth Millbay for many years, but when Millbay was badly damaged by enemy action during World War II the original South Devon Railway station was closed to passenger traffic. Thereafter, North Road became the southern 'terminus' of the branch service from Launceston - though many trains continued to run through to Millbay station as empty stock workings after the withdrawal of passenger facilities in 1941.

Plymouth Mutley

Departing from Plymouth North Road, branch trains ran along the South Devon main line for a distance of 2 miles 66 chains. In the years before World War II, Launceston services called intermediately at the suburban station known as Plymouth Mutley - however, this practice ceased following the closure of the latter station in July 1939.

Situated in a heavily built-up area, Plymouth Mutley was a passenger-only stopping place with no sidings or goods facilities of any kind. There were two platforms, the main station buildings being sited on the up side. The down side platform was equipped with a smaller waiting room and toilet block, and the two platforms were linked by a standard Great Western covered footbridge. Until 1908 Mutley had boasted its own signal box, but this cabin became an early victim of rationalisation, and the signals were, thereafter, controlled from Plymouth North Road East box.

From Plymouth Mutley, trains plunged into the smokey depths of Mutley tunnel, beyond which the double track main line continued due east towards Laira. Before that, however, branch trains clattered through Lipson Vale Halt; this simple wooden halt was equipped with standard Great Western pagoda sheds, and it catered for the residents of another heavily built-up area of Plymouth. The halt (which was not normally served by Launceston trains) was closed in March 1942.

Laira Junction looking west in 1961. The Plymouth and Dartmoor line crossing has been removed from the up and down main lines. This was to allow the main lines to be raised about 18 in. where the crossing was to increase the speed limit from 40 mph to 60 mph. The new diesel depot in the background is still under construction. Laira Junction signal box contatined a 116-lever frame. *Adrian Vaughan Collection*

A busy scene at Laira Halt. showing a train headed by a steam railmotor. Laira depot's coaling stage can be seen in the extreme top right of this photograph. *Lens of Sutton*

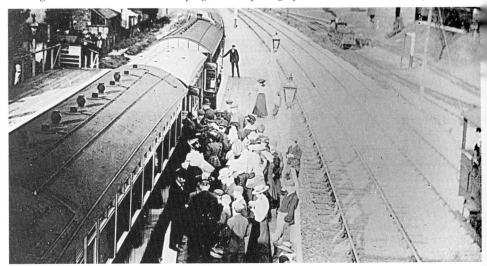

Laira

Reaching Laira, trains passed an extensive motive power depot on the south side of the running lines. Opened in 1901, Laira engine shed was a large 'roundhouse' type depot with an allocation of around 100 locomotives. Engines based here included the usual range of standard Great Western classes, ranging from 'King' class 4-6-0s to the diminutive '1361' class 0-6-0ST dock shunters.

In 1947 the allocation included no less than 12 'Kings', together with 13 'Castle' class 4-6-0s, several 'Hall' class 4-6-0s, a selection of large and small 2-6-2Ts, and the usual assortment of '57XX', '54XX' and '64XX' 0-6-0PTs. The small '44XX' and '45XX' prairies stationed at Laira (at various times) included Nos. 4402, 4407, 4409, 4410, 4524, 4551, 4555, 4568, 4583, 4591, 5541, 5544, 5567, 5569, and 5572, all of which worked on the Launceston or Princetown branches at one time or another.

Laira was also the site of a triangular junction, by means of which LSWR (later Southern Railway) trains could reach Plymouth Friary and Turnchapel, and GWR services could gain access to the Yealmpton branch. The west-to-south arm of this junction diverged from the main line at Lipson Junction, while the south-to-east arm converged at nearby Laira Junction; these junctions also provided access to an extensive system of dock and harbour lines which, in turn, provided connections to numerous private industrial sidings. (A small halt at Laira was closed as long ago as July 1930.)

Tavistock Junction

Having passed Laira Junction, branch trains soon reached Tavistock Junction at which point the Launceston branch diverged northwards from the South Devon main line. Tavistock Junction was the site of an extensive marshalling yard that was greatly expanded to deal with wartime traffic in 1941; this yard was situated on the main line to the east of Tavistock Junction, and it was further enlarged in BR days to provide siding capacity for almost 2,000 wagons. Tavistock Junction marshalling yard was at its peak during the 1960s, but in the following decade the facilities provided here were much reduced, leaving a modest group of parallel sidings on the north side of the main line.

Tavistock Junction marked the start of the Tavistock and Launceston branch proper, and it would be convenient to take this point as the datum for the measurement of distances between Plymouth and Launceston. However, as mentioned above, branch passenger trains worked through from Plymouth Millbay prior to World War II (and from North Road thereafter) and it would be useful to include the following table of distances from Millbay to Tavistock Junction:

	m.	ch.
Plymouth Millbay Station	0	00
Plymouth North Road Passenger Station	0	68
Laira Junction	2	62
Tavistock Junction	3	54

The moving elbows at Tavistock Junction which were operated by lever 56 from the box. The Launceston branch curves sharply away to the left. *L. Crosier*

Marsh Mills station looking south towards Tavistock Junction. This station marked the northern limit of double track working, the two lines disappearing through the arches of the overbridge being signalled for up and down operation. The signal cabin (*left*) was a Saxby & Farmer design, though it later acquired standard GWR roof ventilators. *Rural Publications: Nelson*

Railways in the Marsh Mills Area

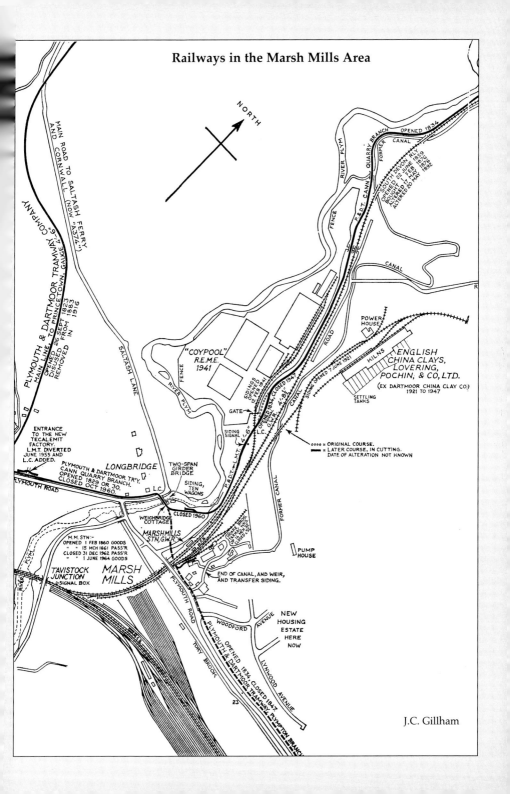

NORTH

PLYMOUTH & DARTMOOR TRAMWAY, 4'-6" COMPANY
MAIN ROAD TO SALTASH FERRY AND CORNWALL (NOW "A.374")
MAIN LINE TO PRINCETOWN, GAUGE 4'-6"
OPENED 26 SEPT. 1823
DISUSED FROM 1883
REMOVED IN 1916

P.&D.T. CANN. QUARRY BRANCH   OPENED 1834

RIVER PLYM
FORMER   CANAL
SOUTH DEVON RLY.
OPENED 22 JUNE 1859
BOUGHT 1 FEB. 1876
ALTERED 1 MAY 1876
ALTERED 20 MAY 1892

FENCE

CANAL

RIVER PLYM

CANAL

POWER
HOUSE

KILNS

ENGLISH
CHINA CLAYS,
LOVERING,
POCHIN, & CO, LTD.
(EX DARTMOOR CHINA CLAY CO.)
1921 TO 1947

"COYPOOL"
R.E.M.E.
1941

SALTASH LANE

FENCE

RIVER PLYM

SIDING OPENED 7 JUNE 1921

SIDING SD.
OP. 12 FEB. 1941

SIDING OPENED 1834. CLOSED 1941

CANAL

G.W.R. 4'-8½"

SETTLING
TANKS

ROAD

GATE

SIDING
SIGNAL

4'-6" L.C.

ROAD

oooo = ORIGINAL COURSE.
▬ = LATER COURSE, IN CUTTING.
DATE OF ALTERATION NOT KNOWN

ENTRANCE
TO THE NEW
TECALEMIT
FACTORY.
L.M.T. DIVERTED
JUNE 1955 AND
L.C. ADDED.

PLYMOUTH & DARTMOOR TR'Y.
CANN. QUARRY BRANCH.
OPENED 1829 OR 30.
CLOSED OCT. 1960.

LONGBRIDGE

TWO-SPAN
GIRDER
BRIDGE

P.&D.T. L.M.T.

FORMER CANAL

PLYMOUTH ROAD

L.C.

SIDING,
TEN
WAGONS

CLOSED 1960

WEIGHBRIDGE
COTTAGE

MARSHMILLS
STN, G.W.R.

H.M. STN:-
OPENED 1 FEB 1860 GOODS
" " 15 MCH 1861 PASS'R
CLOSED 31 DEC 1962 PASS'R
" " 1 JUNE 1964 GOODS

PUMP
HOUSE

TAVISTOCK
JUNCTION
SIGNAL BOX

MARSH
MILLS

RIVER PLYM

PLYMOUTH ROAD

END OF CANAL, AND WEIR,
AND TRANSFER SIDING.

WOODFORD   AVENUE

NEW
HOUSING
ESTATE
HERE
NOW

TORY BROOK

PLYMOUTH & DARTMOOR TRAMWAY PLYMPTON BRANCH
OPENED 1834, CLOSED 1847

LYNWOOD   AVENUE

23

J.C. Gillham

It should also be noted that, although branch trains running between Plymouth and Launceston were, quite logically, designated 'down' workings, they ran on the *up* main line as far as Tavistock Junction. A similar situation pertained in the reverse direction, in that southbound branch trains were regarded as up workings until they reached the end of the branch at Tavistock Junction; on reaching the main line, however, they continued westwards to Plymouth in the 'down' direction in relation to main line traffic.

Marsh Mills

Curving northwards onto the former South Devon & Tavistock line, branch trains continued along a double track section as far as the first intermediate station at Marsh Mills, some 3 miles 72 chains from Plymouth Millbay but only 18 chains from the start of the branch proper at Tavistock Junction.

The passenger station at Marsh Mills was not opened until 15th March, 1861, though goods traffic had been accepted since 1st February, 1860. The station was equipped with up and down platforms, the main booking office and waiting rooms being on the down (northbound) side, while the up platform was provided with a somewhat smaller waiting room.

The buildings here were of simple, but attractive design. They were constructed of local stone laid in decorative 'snecked' courses, with more or less regular courses interrupted, at intervals, by larger blocks of stone. Higher quality stonework was used as dressings around the door and window apertures, and as quoins at the corners of the two buildings. The roofs were double-pitched, and covered in grey slate, the gable ends being finished off with plain barge boards.

These unobtrusive structures had probably been designed by Peter J. Margary, who acted as Engineer to both the South Devon and the Cornwall railways, and later served as GWR Divisional Engineer at Plymouth; substantially similar buildings were erected by Margary at Praze on the Helston branch, and it seems likely that Marsh Mills and Praze stations had been built from the same set of drawings.

Marsh Mills was signalled from a hip-roofed signal cabin on the up platform. This two-storey structure was of typical Saxby & Farmer design, with a brick locking room and rear wall; internally, it contained a 32-lever frame. As the station was situated on a 1 in 100 rising gradient towards Tavistock, a runaway catchpoint was fitted at the north end of the down platform line; these points

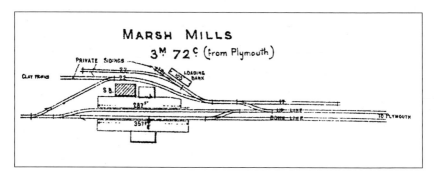

MARSH MILLS

3^M 72^C (from Plymouth)

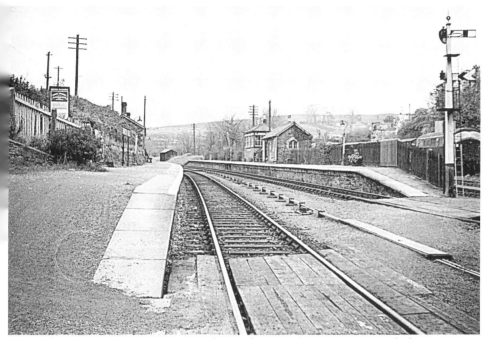

Marsh Mills station in 1962 looking north from the footpath/barrow crossing which provided the only access to the down platform. In the sidings a North British type '2' 'D63XX' class diesel-hydraulic can be seen. The up platform (*left*) was 287 ft long, while the down platform (*right*) had a length of 357 ft. *M. Daly*

'2021' class 0-6-0PT No. 2116 is seen arriving at Marsh Mills with a southbound goods train. Note the Hoare Brothers private owner wagon in the siding; Hoare Brothers had a private siding at Marsh Mills. *G. Sheppard Collection*

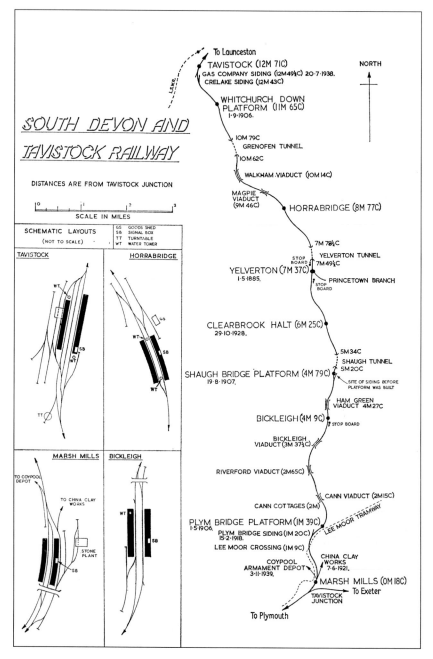

SOUTH DEVON AND

TAVISTOCK RAILWAY

DISTANCES ARE FROM TAVISTOCK JUNCTION

To Launceston
TAVISTOCK (12M 71C)
GAS COMPANY SIDING (12M49½C) 20·7·1938.
CRELAKE SIDING (12M 43C)

NORTH

WHITCHURCH DOWN
PLATFORM (11M 65C)
1·9·1906.

10M 79C
GRENOFEN TUNNEL
10M 62C

WALKHAM·VIADUCT (10M 14C)

MAGPIE
VIADUCT
(9M 46C)

HORRABRIDGE (8M 77C)

7M 78½C

STOP
BOARD

YELVERTON TUNNEL
7M 49½C

YELVERTON (7M 37C)
1·5·1885.

PRINCETOWN BRANCH
STOP
BOARD

CLEARBROOK HALT (6M 25C)
29·10·1928.

5M 34C
SHAUGH TUNNEL
5M 20C

SHAUGH BRIDGE PLATFORM (4M 79C)
19·8·1907.

SITE OF SIDING BEFORE
PLATFORM WAS BUILT

HAM GREEN
VIADUCT 4M 27C

BICKLEIGH (4M 9C)
STOP BOARD

BICKLEIGH
VIADUCT (3M 37½C)

RIVERFORD VIADUCT (2M65C)

CANN VIADUCT (2M15C)

CANN COTTAGES (2M)

LEE MOOR TRAMWAY

PLYM BRIDGE PLATFORM (1M 39C)
1·5·1906.
PLYM BRIDGE SIDING (1M 20C)
15·2·1918.
LEE MOOR CROSSING (1M 9C)

CHINA CLAY
WORKS
7·6·1921.

COYPOOL
ARMAMENT DEPOT
3·11·1939.

MARSH MILLS (0M 18C)
To Exeter
TAVISTOCK
JUNCTION

To Plymouth

SCALE IN MILES

0   1   2   3

SCHEMATIC LAYOUTS	GS	GOODS SHED
(NOT TO SCALE)	SB	SIGNAL BOX
	TT	TURNTABLE
	WT	WATER TOWER

TAVISTOCK

HORRABRIDGE

WT

SB
WT

TT

GS

WT

SB

WT

MARSH MILLS

BICKLEIGH

TO COYPOOL
DEPOT

TO CHINA CLAY
WORKS

TO CHINA CLAY
WORKS

STONE
PLANT

SB

WT

SB

R.E. Taylor and E.R. Shepherd

were connected to the signal box, and signalmen were instructed not to reverse the up main facing points, or allow the single line to be occupied for shunting purposes until the 'train out of section' signal had been received from Bickleigh. The Great Western Railway classified its signal boxes by reference to a complex 'marks' system, the rates of pay for signalmen working in each box being governed by the number of marks awarded for specified duties such pulling the levers, sending bell code signals and working level crossing gates; large boxes at busy main line stations obviously warranted high marks scores, but branch line cabins such as Marsh Mills or Lifton were invariably placed in the lowest classes (4 or 5). At Marsh Mills, the signal box was a class 5 box with 36 marks in 1923, but its score had increased to 52 marks by 1937. However, in 1951 the class 5 classification was abolished, and Marsh Mills box was then up-graded to class 4.

The public goods facilities at Marsh Mills were limited, no cattle pens, end-loading docks, yard crane or goods shed being provided. On the other hand, Marsh Mills was the focal point for a variety of private sidings and industrial lines - the earliest of which predated the South Devon & Tavistock Railway by over 20 years.

The story of these early lines is surprisingly complex. Railway development in the area began in the early 19th century, the first line to open being the 4 ft 6 in. gauge Plymouth & Dartmoor Railway (P&DR), which was completed from Crabtree (Laira) to King Tor on 26th September, 1823 and extended to Sutton Harbour in 1825. As this new line did not serve the Cann Quarry, the Earl of Morley constructed a two mile canal from the quarry workings to the River Plym at Marsh Mills, with a short 4 ft 6 in. gauge connecting tramway between Marsh Mills and the Plymouth & Dartmoor line at Crabtree. The canal and its tramway link were opened at the end of 1829, and in 1834 the tramway was extended eastwards from Marsh Mills to Plympton.

For a time, Marsh Mills became a transhipment point between rail and water transport, but the advantages of a direct rail link to Cann Quarry soon became obvious, and in 1834 (or thereabouts) the Cann Quarry branch was extended northwards alongside the canal to reach the quarry; the superseded waterway then became a mill leat.

A further development occurred in the 1850s when, as we have seen, a 4 ft 6 in. gauge branch was constructed from Plym Bridge to the Lee Moor clayworks. This line, which formed a connection with the earlier Cann Quarry branch of the P&DR at Plym Bridge, was modestly successful, and when the Plymouth & Dartmoor main line fell out of use during the 1880s the Lee Moor Tramway continued to operate in conjunction with the Cann Quarry branch - both sections of route being known as 'The Lee Moor Tramway' (although in reality only the northern portion of this 4 ft 6 in. gauge industrial line was the LMT).

The Cann Quarry/Lee Moor route was worked mainly by horses, although two small Peckett 0-4-0STs were used on the upper part of the line above Plym Bridge. The tramway converged with the GWR line just beyond Marsh Mills passenger station, and then ran beside the 'main line' for a considerable distance; a glance at the map on page 83 will give some idea of the complexity of the railway system in and around Marsh Mills, and the location of some of the industrial premises mentioned in the text will also be readily apparent.

In the early days of the railway, about 1888, a flour mill occupied a site near the station, and much traffic in truck loads was despatched to Devon and Cornish stations over a period of forty years.

In 1921 the Dartmoor China Clay Company had settling tanks at nearby Woodford, and private siding facilities were provided on 7th June, 1921. The company was taken over by English Clays Lovering Pochin & Company Limited in 1947. The production of china clay, piped from Lee Moor after the closure of the Lee Moor Tramway, increased considerably and the siding accommodation was extended. This clay, which was of the highest grade, was being produced at well over 200,000 tons a year during the 1970s and there was a heavy rail traffic from the works to Fowey for shipment, and to stations in the Potteries.

In 1932, Hoare Brothers of Tavistock developed their Tarmac Works at Marsh Mills, and there was a regular daily traffic of roadstone of all grades from the firm's Pitt's Cleave Quarry near Tavistock, conveyed in 20-ton privately owned hopper wagons. The works closed in 1952.

Hoare Brothers' tarmac works and the Dartmoor China Clay Company sidings were situated on the up side of the running lines. Access from the main line was arranged by means of a goods loop line that passed behind the up platform, and it was thus possible for these private sidings to be shunted without interfering with the main line. The China Clay company's sidings were part of an extensive system of private lines, and in the 1960s a privately-owned diesel shunting locomotive was employed to position china clay wagons in the various works sidings.

If, for any reason, the clay firm's engine was not available for shunting duties, a BR locomotive was sent out to the clay sidings to perform this work.

New siding accommodation to a Government Establishment was opened on 3rd November, 1939, and this facility dealt with much traffic during the remainder of the war. The traffic continued during the immediate post-war period and the accommodation was still in use during the 1970s. A new ground frame on the down side of the Lee Moor Tramway, 330 yards from Marsh Mills signal box, where the tramway crossed the depot line, with up and down signals protecting the crossing, was brought into use on 12th February, 1941.

The Ministry of Defence sidings were situated on the west side of the line, and they were entered via a connection that was facing to down trains. The MoD private line continued northwards alongside the main line for a considerable distance, the 4 ft 6 in. gauge Lee Moor Tramway being situated between the running line and the Ministry of Defence branch.

Before 1892, Marsh Mills had the distinction of being served by three different gauges of line. First came the 4 ft 6 in. gauge of the Cann Quarry line (the Dartmoor gauge); next the 7 ft 0¼ in. gauge of the South Devon & Tavistock Railway, and in 1876 the standard gauge of 4 ft 8½ in. when the third rail was laid to enable trains of the London & South Western Company to run from Lydford to Devonport via Tavistock and Marsh Mills.

There was an incline of 1 in 60 rising for about 4 miles towards Bickleigh, with a stop board at 4 miles 6 chains for up freight trains.

Assisting engines were placed behind down freight trains at Marsh Mills, and

'64XX' class 0-6-0PT No. 6430 leaves Marsh Mills with the 2.10 pm Plymouth to Tavistock South train on 22nd December, 1962. *Peter W. Gray*

Lee Moor Crossing looking south in 1933, showing the 4 ft 6 in. 'Dartmoor Gauge' crossing on the level near Plym Bridge. The tramway was deep ballasted to assist the horses; the short siding visible to the left functioned as a trap point for runaway tramway wagons. *R.W. Kidner*

pushed their trains to Yelverton uncoupled; if such engines were required to go beyond Yelverton they had to be attached to the front of the train at Yelverton.

The passenger station closed on 31st December, 1962, but public goods traffic continued to be dealt with at Marsh Mills until 1st June, 1964.

The Marsh Mills-Bickleigh electric staff working was replaced by electric token on 2nd May, 1956; the signal box was closed, the signals removed and the points altered to hand operation on 4th April, 1965, upon which date the branch connection to the main line at Tavistock Junction was removed and replaced by a new single connecting line from No. 4 road in the yard to Marsh Mills.

Lee Moor Tramway Crossing

Leaving Marsh Mills, down branch trains resumed their ascent towards Yelverton, and with the Lee Moor Tramway maintaining a roughly parallel course on the left hand side of the line, the route continued northwards towards Lee Moor Crossing, at which point the tramway crossed from the west to the east side of the branch by means of a 'diamond' crossing.

Situated 1 mile 9 chains from Tavistock Junction, the tramway crossing was provided with a signal box and up and down home and distant signals. The up home signal was 40 yards from the box while the up distant was situated some 970 yards from the cabin; the corresponding distances for the down home and down distant signals were 50 yards and 710 yards respectively. One of the levers in the box worked trap points on the tramway, and this ensured that runaway wagons on the 4 ft 6 in. gauge horse-worked line would not foul the GWR 'main line'.

Lee Moor Crossing signal cabin was a small, single storey box with a five-lever GWR stud locking frame. The box itself had originally been erected at Tavistock, but this semi-prefabricated structure was moved from Tavistock following re-signalling work carried out at that station in 1895.

As the crossing box was not a block post it had no instruments, but the gateman was provided with an electric indicator and a bell, which was worked by a pointer on the instrument in Bickleigh box, and showed when trains had left Bickleigh or Marsh Mills stations. Once the indicator showed 'down train on line' or 'up train on line', no tramway vehicles were allowed to cross the main line until the train had safely passed. Assuming, however, that no main line trains were due, the gateman was instructed to place his up and down signals at danger during movements over the tramway crossing.

The tramway was extensively used for conveyance of china clay loaded in 4 ton wagons drawn by horses, from Lee Moor Clay Works to Sutton Harbour for shipment. The usual load was four or five trucks drawn by two horses.

The tramway was closed between Lee Moor and Marsh Mills in 1947, but the crossing remained in normal 'use' until January 1955 when the signals were taken out of use, the catch-points on either side of the crossing secured in the 'open' position, and the gateman was withdrawn.

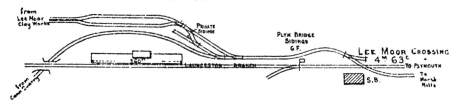

PLYM BRIDGE PLATFORM
5ᴹ 13ᶜ

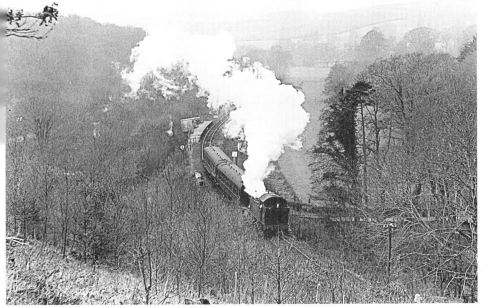

Above: '45XX' class 2-6-2T No.5544 leaves Plym Bridge Platform with the 10.40 am Plymouth to Launceston, 17th March, 1962.   *Peter W. Gray*

Left: The Launceston branch crossing the Cann Quarry canal near Plym Bridge *c.* 1930. Note that the stone blocks carrying the rails of the Plymouth & Dartmoor Cann Wood branch along the towpath are in many instances still in place.
R.W. Kidner Collection

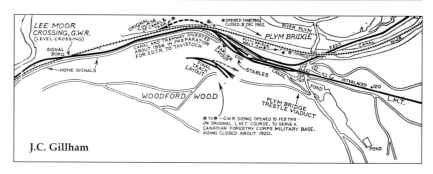

J.C. Gillham

Plym Bridge Platform

Continuing northwards through picturesque, well-wooded scenery, the branch reached the site of an abandoned siding on the down side of the line at 1 mile 20 chains. Brought into use on 15th February, 1918, this siding was used by the Canadian Forestry Commission for the loading of timber, mainly pit-props, which were obtained from the adjacent woods. The siding was controlled from a ground frame, locked by key on the electric train staff. It was closed about 1920, and reopened for a short time on 13th July, 1922. The date of its final removal is not recorded.

Beyond, the line ascended to Plym Bridge Platform. Situated at 1 mile 39 chains, on a rising gradient of 1 in 97, this simple platform, of all wooden construction, was opened on 1st May, 1906. Plym Bridge remained in use until May 1949, when its length was reduced by 100 ft and it was reconstructed in pre-cast concrete. The work was completed in October 1949. It was closed with effect from 31st December, 1962.

Surrounded by beautiful woods, the halt was used by thousands of people from Plymouth at week ends, who were conveyed by ordinary trains as well as by special auto services on Bank Holidays - these being permitted to work to and from Marsh Mills under special signalling instructions.

From Plym Bridge Platform, the railway traversed an embankment as it climbed steadily through Cann Woods on a 1 in 60 rising gradient. At 2 miles 0 chains, near Cann Cottages, the lineside loading of firewood was specially authorised as from 18th December, 1921.

The Cann Quarry branch of the Plymouth & Dartmoor Railway extended for about half a mile beyond Plym Bridge. It was opened on 20th November, 1829 and remained in use until 1855.

Between Plym Bridge Platform and Bickleigh there were three closely-spaced viaducts, namely the Cann and Riverford Viaducts at 2 miles 15 chains and 2 miles 65 chains respectively, followed by Bickleigh Viaduct at 3 miles 37½ chains.

The Cann Viaduct was originally a wooden trestle structure resting on stone piers, but it was rebuilt between 2nd February, 1905 and 10th March, 1907, the new viaduct being a six-arch structure built of Staffordshire blue brick. It was 127 yds long and 63 ft high.

The neighbouring Riverford Viaduct, with five granite arches, was 197 ft long

'45XX' class 2-6-2T No. 4566 crosses the 6-arch Cann viaduct with the 10.15 am Launceston to Plymouth working on 17th March, 1962. *Peter W. Gray*

'57XX' class 0-6-0PT No. 4658 on the 5-arch Riverford viaduct with the 12.40 pm service from Tavistock to Plymouth on 17th March, 1962. *Peter W. Gray*

'45XX' class 2-6-2T No. 5544 leaves Bickleigh viaduct with the 12.40 pm Launceston to Plymouth, 17th March, 1962. The rebuilt viaduct had seven masonry spans; the piers of the original timber viaduct can be seen beside the new bridge.   *Peter W. Gray*

This postcard view of Bickleigh looking towards Plymouth shows the station pre-World War I with the second Bickleigh signal box in use at the south end of the crossing loop.
                                                                                                                P. Strong Collection

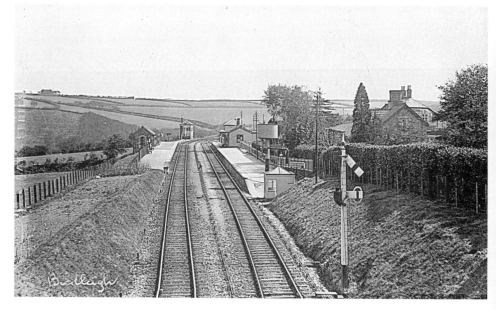

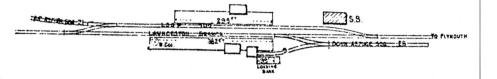

BICKLEIGH
7ᴹ 63ᶜ

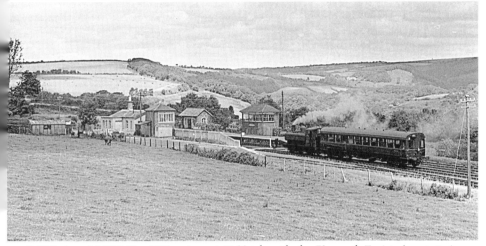

'64XX' class 0-6-0PT No. 6438 arrives at Bickleigh with the Plymouth-Tavistock auto-train service, 4th August, 1962. The third signal box can be seen to the left of the locomotive; this was built around 1913.   *Peter W. Gray*

'64XX' class 0-6-0PT No. 6400 stands at Bickleigh while passengers board the auto-train service to Tavistock in 1962.   *M. Daly*

and 97 ft high, and had a length of 127 ft. It was brought into use on 12th March, 1893 when the original timber viaduct was superseded.

Bickleigh Viaduct, of seven arches, was 167 yds long and 123 ft high, and it was brought into use at the same time as the rebuilt Riverford Viaduct on 12th March, 1893.

Bickleigh

Bickleigh, the next station, was 7 miles 63 chains from Plymouth Millbay and 4 miles 9 chains from the start of the branch at Tavistock Junction. It was situated on a rising gradient of 1 in 60, and had been opened for passenger traffic on 22nd June, 1859; goods traffic was handled from 1st February, 1860.

Bickleigh was a crossing station with up and down platforms. The main station building was on the down side, and there was a small waiting room on the up platform. The main building was a gable-roofed structure of typical broad gauge design, with a tall chimney and a small platform canopy; the up side building was of superficially similar appearance, but on closer examination it became apparent that the two buildings were built to differing designs - the up side shelter being a gothic-style structure whereas its counterpart on the down platform was of Italianate appearance. This suggests that the up side building was erected at a slightly later date (probably in the 1860s, after P.J. Margary had assumed responsibility for engineering work on the Launceston and Tavistock line).

At first glance, it seemed that Bickleigh had two signal boxes, but in reality there was only one - a two-storey hip-roofed box on the down platform having been superseded by a new GWR box on the up side at an early date. The old signal cabin then found a new lease of life as a goods store, though its outward appearance remained unchanged. A third box was built on a new site in 1913.

The new signal box contained a 23-lever frame, and it was better-sited to afford signalmen an unobstructed view in each direction. The box was a class 5 box with 47 marks until 1951, after which it became class 4.

The up and down loop lines at Bickleigh were 980 and 904 ft long respectively but the down crossing loop could only hold trains of 38 wagons between the down starting signal and the catch points at the Plymouth end of the loop. If time allowed for such a manoeuvre, long freight trains would be shunted towards the down refuge siding, but if 'line clear' had been given for an up train to enter the station the down working would be held at the down home signal if it was too long for the loop.

Minor details at Bickleigh included cattle pens, loading docks, and a 'mushroom' type water tank at the north end of the down platform. The two platforms were originally fenced with traditional pale-and-space fencing, and at night the station was lit by oil lamps resting in tapered glass lanterns.

In the early days of the railway the station was frequently used by the Lopes family, the station house being employed as a waiting room. A stable was attached for the horses from the estate.

After the closing of Shaugh siding Bickleigh station dealt with considerable quantities of china clay traffic from pits in the Shaugh area. This clay, in suspension, was washed down a two mile pipe line to drying sheds at Shaugh Bridge.

Departing from Bickleigh, down trains passed beneath a road overbridge at the north end of the station, and with the up refuge siding running parallel to the right, the scenic journey to Launceston resumed. Passing through a cutting, the line emerged onto the lofty Ham Green Viaduct (4 miles 27 chains). Built as a replacement for the original timber viaduct, Ham Green Viaduct was a six-arch structure that stood 91 ft above local ground level at its highest point. It was 190 yds long, and was brought into use on 19th November, 1899.

Shaugh Bridge Platform

Still heading northwards, the line continued to Shaugh Bridge Platform. Situated at 4 miles 79 chains, this was probably the site of a works siding used during the construction of Shaugh tunnel, reopened on 1st August, 1870 for loading low grade iron ore produced at a mine below Shaugh bridge on the east side of the river. The iron ore was forwarded to Plymouth for shipment to South Wales for smelting. The mine had a recorded output of 4,670 tons between 1870 and 1874.

It was the original intention to connect the South Devon & Tavistock Railway with the quarry workings in the Dewerstone area. Granite trackways led to the various workings which were extended to an embankment, completed except for a granite arch which would have spanned the River Plym, but permission to build across the river could not be obtained and the scheme was then abandoned. The loss of the embankment was a serious blow to the quarry communications, but the extension of the tracks to the river made possible the removal of some granite by road to the rail head at Shaugh siding.

A platform halt was opened for passengers at Shaugh Bridge on 19th August, 1907, and, this new stopping place was extensively used by passengers from Plymouth who flocked to the surrounding woods and to the famous Dewerstone Rock rising over 600 feet on the southern edge of Dartmoor.

On Bank Holidays and other special occasions during the summer period rail auto-cars were permitted to work from Bickleigh to Shaugh Bridge Platform and back without having to go through the section to Yelverton. This working was covered by a special signalling regulation.

Shaugh Bridge Platform was on the down side of the line, and its long, curving platform was linked to an adjacent road overbridge by a sloping earth and cinder path, by means of which travellers could ascend to road level. Its facilities consisted of a 'pagoda' shelter, one or two platform seats, and a large nameboard bearing the words 'SHAUGH BRIDGE'.

The pagoda shed was built of corrugated iron sheeting, and its overall dimensions, at ground level, were approximately 20 ft x 8 ft. The halt was lit by oil lamps resting in traditional glass lanterns, and its immediate surroundings were attractively planted with trees and shrubs. For administration purposes Shaugh Bridge was supervised by the station master at nearby Bickleigh. The halt was closed to all traffic on and from 31st December, 1962.

Shaugh Bridge Platform on 13th June, 1926. This simple halt was at one time used as a terminal point for special push-pull working from Plymouth. *H.C. Casserley*

A group of scouts look on as their train, the 10.15 am Launceston to Plymouth, pulls into Clearbrook Halt, 4th August, 1962. *Peter W. Gray*

Clearbrook Halt

Departing from Shaugh Bridge Platform, trains climbed northwards, through spectacular moorland scenery, on a relentless 1 in 58 rising gradient. With the sharp exhaust beats of the labouring engine leaving no doubt that the general direction was still upwards, trains thundered through the 308 yds-long Shaugh Tunnel, which commenced at 5 miles 20 chains and ended at 5 miles 34 chains. Emerging into daylight once again, the route snaked its way along the Meavy valley on a low embankment towards Clearbrook Halt.

This halt, at 6 miles 25 chains, was opened on 29th October, 1928, and it remained in use until the line was closed on and from 31st December, 1962. It served a small community in the nearby village of Clearbrook, and also provided transport facilities for people in the hamlets of Hoo-Meavy and Good-a-Meavy.

The halt was sited on the down side of the running line, and its platform was formed of earth-and-cinder infill held in place by old sleepers and upright lengths of old Barlow-type bridge rail. Passenger accommodation consisted of an arc-roofed corrugated iron shelter and a platform seat. The platform was lit by simple oil lamps, and for administrative purposes this unstaffed stopping place came under the supervision of the Yelverton station master.

The rising gradients continued beyond the halt as far as 1 mile 32 chains, at which point a stop board was provided for up goods trains.

In 1885 an accident occurred at milepost 6 when an engine and coach were derailed and toppled over a bank. The engine was LSWR '395' class 0-6-0 No. 442, working the 4.0 pm stopping train from Exeter to Plymouth. The cause of the accident was a broken coupling. This engine, built by Neilson of Glasgow (works No. 2266) afterwards worked in the Exeter area for forty years. It was withdrawn from service in May 1961.

Yelverton

Having reached the top of the aforementioned incline, down workings entered the important intermediate station at Yelverton, which was 11 miles 11 chains from Plymouth Millbay and 7 miles 37 chains from Tavistock Junction.

Before the opening of the Princetown Railway on 11th August, 1883, Yelverton had siding accommodation only for full truck load traffic. A petition by local inhabitants for a passenger station, made in the early days of the railway, was turned down on the grounds that the cost of one porter would be more than the traffic could bear!

When trains first ran to and from Princetown, they travelled northwards over the mixed gauge between Yelverton and Horrabridge for connecting purposes until 1st May, 1885, when a passenger station was opened at Yelverton. This saw the commencement of a rapid development in the Yelverton area. The station was 500 ft above sea level, and the village itself some 100 ft higher. The position was very bracing, within easy reach of Plymouth, and had a good train service.

By 1913, Yelverton was the second busiest station on the line so far as originating passenger traffic was concerned, and possibly the busiest when all

A postcard view of Yelverton across the fields from the south towards the station.   All is quiet on the Plymouth-Tavistock line but a Princetown branch train can be seen beyond.

P. Strong Collection

An attractive turn of the century view of Yelverton station, looking northwards towards Yelverton tunnel. The unusual 5-sided up side building can be seen to the right.   *L&GRP*

Yelverton station and station approach with the Princetown branch curving sharply away to the left behind the up platform.

P. Strong Collection

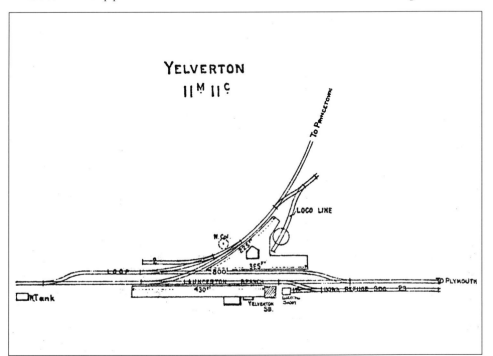

Passengers can be seen awaiting the arrival of a Plymouth-bound train in this Edwardian era view. Meanwhile a goods train from the Princetown branch waits at the signal.   *L&GRP*

The 10.40 am Plymouth-Tavistock service stands at Yelverton station awaiting the arrival of a train for Plymouth, 1st March, 1956.   *R.M. Casserley*

Yelverton station looking south towards Plymouth, with the signal box and down refuge siding on the right. The gabled signal box was typical of those erected by the GWR in the 1890s.
Rural Publications: Nelson

A view northwards along Yelverton station down platform towards the tunnel. Note the steep gradient through the tunnel. By the time this photograph was taken the connection to the Princetown branch had been removed. The down platform was 430 ft long.
Rural Publications: Nelson

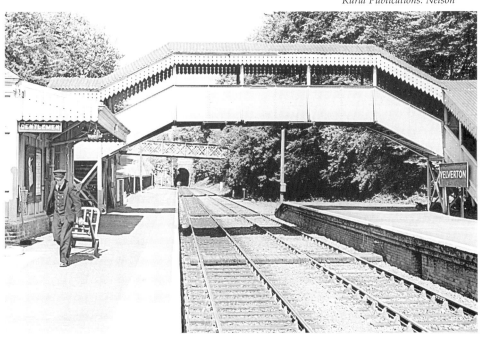

Nature quickly reclaimed the trackbed of the Princetown branch platform after the removal of the track in the 1950s.   *Rural Publications: Nelson*

'45XX' class 2-6-2T No. 4590 emerges from Yelverton tunnel with the 10.15 am from Launceston, 2nd March, 1954.   *Peter W. Gray*

passenger traffic was taken into account. At the turn of the century the station had its own bookstall and the station forecourt was a scene of great activity, with horse-drawn vehicles conveying passengers to and from the station.

Yelverton was, in many ways, an unusual station. It had up and down platforms for Plymouth to Launceston traffic, with a third platform for Princetown branch trains on the up side. The branch platform formed, with the up main line, a triangular arrangement - these two platforms being neatly sited in the 'V' junction between the main line and the branch.

The up and down sides of the station were linked by a typical Great Western covered footbridge, and the station buildings on each platform were timber-framed structures with prominent external framing. The up side building was five-sided, while the down side booking office and waiting room was a conventional, hip-roofed building with a projecting platform canopy.

The signal box, sited at the south end of the down platform, was a gable-roof design with a 35-lever frame. Other buildings at Yelverton included a standard GWR pagoda shed on the down platform, together with the usual assortment of huts, sheds and stores.

There was no run-round facility for Princetown branch trains at Yelverton, and for this reason gravity working was resorted to when branch trains had set down their passengers (*see Chapter Nine* for further details of the Princetown line).

Like other country stations, Yelverton was a significant centre of employment in a rural area, its station master being a figure of some importance in the local community. In the early 1930s the station master here was Mr W.J. Roberts, but he moved to a new position at Bugle in 1934, and Mr E.T. Roberts (possibly a relative) came from Ashburton to replace him.

Yelverton was equipped with a 23 ft 6 in. diameter turntable for the Princetown branch engines, and had up and down crossing loops each 719 ft long. The branch platform was shortened, the connection from the down loop to the branch line removed and the curve improved on 22nd May, 1933. A connection from the up main line to the branch was put out of use on 28th April, 1957. The signal box was closed, the signals disconnected, the down line converted to a single line, the up line secured and closed and the electric token section between Horrabridge and Bickleigh brought into use, all on 4th May, 1959.

A stop board for down freight trains was provided at the top of the 1 in 60 gradient, falling for 1½ miles towards Horrabridge. The speed of freight trains over this incline was restricted to 20 mph.

The station was in a delightful setting with rhododendron trees in profusion, and many rose bushes on the platform. It was kept in beautiful condition and was the pride of the staff and the delight of the commuters.

Yelverton tunnel commenced at 7 miles 49 chains and was 641 yds long. It was so straight that daylight could be seen through it when viewed from the station platform.

Yelverton marked the summit of the South Devon & Tavistock section, and the next two and a half miles were marked by a succession of favourable gradients.

Yelverton tunnel was sited on a 1 in 110 falling gradient, but having emerged from the northern portal of the tunnel, down trains descended towards Horrabridge at 1 in 60.

A busy scene looking north as an up train arrives at Horrabridge around the turn of the century. The down platform (*left*) had a length of 345 ft. *Lens of Sutton*

A general view of Horrabridge looking south, with the up siding visible to the left and the 230 ft up platform in the middle distance. A 16-ton mineral wagon is prominent on the extreme left. *Rural Publications: Nelson*

Horrabridge

Heading north-westwards, the railway was carried across the main A386 road on an impressive girder bridge, and the single line then doubled to form a passing loop as it entered Horrabridge station.

Horrabridge, 8 miles 77 chains from Tavistock Junction, was opened on 22nd June, 1859 to passenger traffic, and on 1st February, 1860 for goods. It closed to both from 31st December, 1962. The station served a wide area and dealt with a heavy coal and agricultural traffic. Its passenger traffic remained fairly constant over a long period, and was the least affected by the large decrease in numbers suffered by other stations when the bus services started to operate in the early 1920s.

It was a busy place in the 1860s, when it handled large quantities of copper ore from the local mines, forwarded to Plymouth for shipment. Several requests were made at the half-yearly meetings of the company for better road access and improved loading facilities to avoid delays which were then taking place in despatching the copper traffic - from two or three hundred tons a month - and which had been previously conveyed by the Tavistock Canal.

Horrabridge was a crossing station with an up loop 397 feet long and a down loop of 442 feet. Public level crossing gates, said to have had the longest single span in the country, were abolished (except for a wicket gate), and the crossing closed to traffic on 5th March, 1952.

The station was on an incline of 1 in 60, and special precautions had to be taken to secure detached vehicles. Goods trains had to be placed in sidings before station work commenced.

The track layout at Horrabridge included up and down refuge sidings, the up siding having a capacity of 44 wagons while the down refuge line could accommodate 35 vehicles. The up siding formed a headshunt for the goods shed siding, and a similar situation pertained on the down side of the line - the down refuge siding being used as a headshunt when wagons were shunted into a short goods siding on the west side of the station.

The main station building at Horrabridge was on the up side. like its counterpart at Bickleigh, it was a 'Brunelian' gable-roofed structure of vaguely-Italianate appearance, with a tall chimney stack and a projecting platform canopy. In contrast to Bickleigh (which was of stone construction) Horrabridge station building was a timber-framed structure clad in horizontal weather boarding, and in this respect it was reminiscent of the wooden 'Brunel' stations originally provided on the Oxford Worcester & Wolverhampton Railway.

Facilities on the down side consisted of a small stone waiting room. Other items of interest here included a goods shed and a Saxby & Farmer type signal box, the latter building being on the up platform beside the main building. Locomotives were able to take water from standard GWR water columns at each end of the crossing loop, and at night the station was lit by gas lamps.

The signal box and station building at Horrabridge as seen from the train on 20th August, 1954. The smaller upper lights above the main windows of the signal box were typical Saxby & Farmer features. *H.C. Casserley*

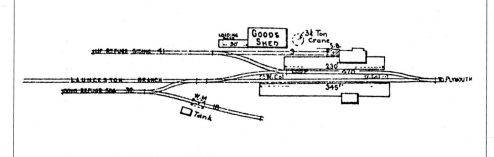

Walkham Viaduct

From Horrabridge, the line dropped on a 1 in 60 descending gradient. Magpie Viaduct, at 9 miles 46 chains, was 216 yds long and 62 ft high. It was rebuilt with four arches in Staffordshire blue brick and brought into use on 8th June, 1902. The remains of the original viaduct could be discerned beside the replacement bridge. Beyond, the railway continued along embankments to the spectacular Walkham Viaduct.

This famous viaduct, 367 yards long and 132 feet high, described as 'the most matured design of Brunel's timber viaducts' was erected to span the valley of the River Walkham, between Horrabridge and Grenofen tunnel. Like all the famous engineer's timber viaducts in Devon and Cornwall, it had great beauty, and fitted gracefully into the local landscape.

The viaduct comprised 15 spans of 66 ft each and two end spans of approximately 59 ft 6 in. each. The superstructure was carried on tall stone piers, with gothic headed openings and buttresses tapering from tip to base. Cast iron tips rested on top of the buttresses from which the timber beams sprang to support the longitudinal timbers. The timber, which came from the Baltic, was very strong, and had an average life of thirty years. It was kyanised as a precaution against fire.

The reconstructed viaduct was brought into use in September 1910. The same number of spans was adhered to and the piers were raised in brickwork to take the bedstones, each weighing six tons, which were lowered into position from a temporary gantry erected at floor level of the old viaduct. The main girders were placed into position on to the bedstones by two twelve-ton cranes, one at each end. This stage of the work was carried out on Sundays.

The cross-girders and rail-bearers were fixed during weekdays, without disturbing the beams carrying the permanent way, the cross-girders being threaded in from the outside by three-ton cranes and the rail-bearers lowered on to cross girders from above by removing portions of the decking, which was eventually replaced by steel flooring for the permanent way.

The girders were conveyed, pair by pair, on 'Crocodile' type bogie well wagons from the maker's works at Horsehay, Shropshire. The work was carried out by the railway's own bridge gangs, under the direction of the Plymouth Engineer, Mr H.D. Smith.

The greatest attention was paid to all viaducts and bridges. Each was examined several times yearly by a bridge gang, each comprising 14 men and 2 look-out men, with a chargeman.

The men would work at great heights and would lower themselves from the decking by means of bowline loops. They were very skilled, and like other grades of railway workers, took a keen pride in their work. The history of Brunel's timber viaducts records no instances of accidents or falling.

Having crossed the viaduct, trains continued, first along embankments, and then through cuttings, to Grenofen tunnel. Situated at 10 miles 62 chains, this tunnel was 374 yds long, and it passed beneath the hamlet of Grenofen.

A view of the second Magpie viaduct shortly after its construction in 1902. *P. Strong Collection*

A train passes over Brunel's famous 15-span timber viaduct at Walkham; it was to survive in this form until reconstruction in 1910. This postcard is incorrectly labelled Magpie Viaduct.

P. Strong Collection

Whitchurch Down Platform

Nearing Tavistock, down trains reached Whitchurch Down Platform (11 miles 65 chains). Sited just 1 mile 6 chains from Tavistock, this platform, on the up side of the line, was opened on 1st September, 1906, and it remained in use until the closure of the line in 1962. The halt served the village of Whitchurch - an outlying suburb of Tavistock, delightfully situated under the shoulder of Whitchurch Down on the edge of Dartmoor.

The halt consisted of a 351 ft-long, brick-faced platform, with an austere corrugated iron shelter for the benefit of local travellers. The platform was lit by gas and fenced with post-and-wire fencing.

Curving north-eastwards, trains reached the site of Crelake siding. This siding, 28 chains from Tavistock station, was brought into use shortly after the opening of the line to deal with copper ore traffic from the adjacent Wheal Crelake Mine; it was well placed for the Tavistock Canal, which had previously conveyed the traffic to Morwellham. The traffic was diverted to rail when the South Devon & Tavistock Railway offered special rates.

The loss of this and other traffic became so serious that the canal company petitioned the Duke of Bedford for assistance to enable them to compete with the railway by reducing the dock dues at Morwellham. This appeal was not successful, and the canal traffic continued to decline up to 1869. Then came an alarming slump in copper production which practically ceased in 1870, causing in turn, loss of revenue to the railway and the closure of the siding in the 1870s. The navigation of the canal ceased in 1873.

Tavistock

A siding for Tavistock Gas Company, contemplated for many years, was provided on 20th July, 1938. Situated on the down side, 21½ chains from Tavistock station, it was worked from a two-lever ground frame locked by key on the train staff. The coal was unloaded from truck to hopper, and by a chute to lorries, which conveyed the coal a short distance to the gas works.

Tavistock gas works siding could accommodate ten wagons, and vehicles could be propelled into the siding from Tavistock station without a brake van, and at a speed not exceeding five miles per hour. The engine had to be kept at the Tavistock end of the wagons during this operation, and the siding was not worked during the hours of darkness or during fog or falling snow.

Situated 16 miles 45 chains from Plymouth Millbay and 12 miles 71 chains from the main line at Tavistock Junction, Tavistock was the most important station on the branch for both passenger and goods traffic. The first public passenger train ran on 22nd June, 1859; the last on 29th December, 1962. Goods traffic facilities operated from 1st December, 1860 until 7th September, 1964. The suffix 'SOUTH' was added to the station name on 26th September, 1949.

The station had a 45 ft diameter engine turntable and two long crossing loops, the up loop being 946 ft long while the down loop had a length of 962 ft. These two loops were separated by a middle line, which was not signalled for through

Whitchurch Down Platform, looking north. *Lens of Sutton*

A Launceston to Laira goods working is seen in the yard at Tavistock South in December 1962. The sheds visible to the left were used as a wool store by Messrs Fulford Perry Spear Ltd. The 60-ton wagon weighbridge can be glimpsed to the right. *M. Daly*

running, but could be used for shunting or stabling purposes.

The up and down platforms were 405 ft and 290 ft long respectively, and there was a commodious goods yard on the down side. The signal box, with 36 levers, was at the south end of the up platform.

The original station was burnt down in the summer of 1887, and was rebuilt on much the same lines but with stone instead of wood. It had the only all-over roof on the line. The station served a large agricultural area. It had a good commuter traffic to Plymouth and was a busy place right up to the time of the introduction of bus services in the early 1920s. Even up to World War II the passenger traffic was good, cheap-day, half-day and evening excursion fares attracting much local traffic to and from Plymouth.

The effect of motor competition was felt less upon this line than upon many other branch lines in the west. There was a good flow of passengers, right up to the beginning of World War II, and this continued until the end of petrol rationing in 1950, which, with the increase in private motoring and in local bus services, caused the traffic to decline seriously.

The freight traffic was heavy; coal, manures and animal feeding stuffs being dealt with in large quantities in the ample siding accommodation provided, while pit-props, granite, wool, livestock, and roadstone formed the bulk of the forwarded traffic. There was a large increase in the latter from 1929 onwards, when Pitt's Cleave Quarry, connected by private siding, came into full production. (*See Chapter Eight* for quarry siding working.)

Tavistock's great day was the second Wednesday in October, when Goose Fair ('Goosey Fair', in the vernacular) was held. This event brought thousands of people to the town from Plymouth, and the last special train from Tavistock, which left at about 11 pm was always crowded with late night revellers, including several who had to be assisted aboard and placed in charge of others who undertook to see them off at their destination station in Plymouth. These crowds were always good-humoured, and responded well to firm persuasion.

During World War II, Tavistock was very busy, many people taking up temporary residence in the town and district to escape from the dangers of heavily-bombed Plymouth. During the heavy raids in March and April 1941, when Plymouth became 'the worst blitzed city' in England, extra trains were run over the branch to convey, not only the regular users, but also the thousands who left Plymouth to spend the night with friends who provided them with temporary accommodation; many people camped in the woods near Bickleigh, Clearbrook and Shaugh during the heaviest raids. The trains were so crowded even upon arrival at Tavistock, that passengers had to move off the platform before others could alight from compartments, luggage and guards vans.

There was a large increase in inward freight traffic during the war period, when many firms transferred from Plymouth to the Tavistock area. Traffic for Government departments was also very heavy, and involved special trains which were dealt with at Pitt's Cleave Quarry. The American Army authorities also dealt with a vast quantity of traffic; on one special occasion in July 1944 for example, over 200 trucks were loaded in one week. There were army camps and depots on the Downs near the town.

A view from the train looking south along the platform at Tavistock South, 20th August, 1954. The up platform can be seen to the left, while the 'middle siding' is visible to the right.

H.C. Casserley

A view from under the overall roof at Tavistock South looking towards Plymouth. The 'middle siding' was used during shunting operations.

Rural Publications: Nelson

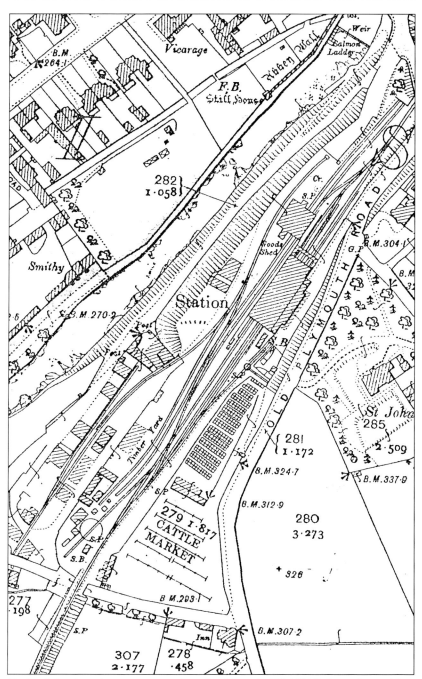

Tavistock South station.   *Reproduced from the 25", 1906 Ordnance Survey Map*

'45XX' class 2-6-2T No. 5541 stands in the up platform at Tavistock with a Launceston to Plymouth train on 2nd May, 1961. The gabled '1890s' style signal box was erected around 1895 as a replacement for two earlier Saxby & Farmer type boxes, one of which was moved to Lee Moor Crossing, while the other (at the south end of the station) found a new use as a Signal & Telegraph department office and store. *R.C. Riley*

'45XX' class 2-6-2T No. 4583 on the 12.12 pm Plymouth to Launceston train at Tavistock South on 13th July, 1956. The goods shed can be seen to the right of the locomotive. *F. Hornby*

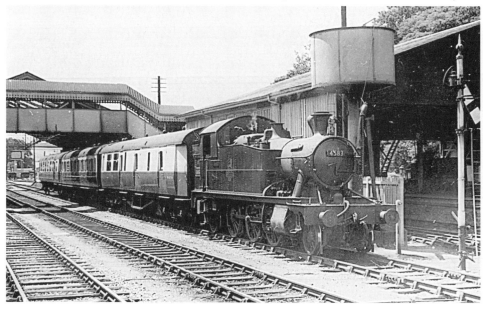

The Tavistock-Lydford electric train staff was replaced by a wooden staff, one engine in steam, in June 1964; all signals, except the up distant (fixed), were removed, but all points were still worked from a ground frame, as from 27th July, 1964. The signal box was one of the few remaining with a single-needle telegraph instrument, a relic of the early days of signalling, before boxes were provided with telephones.

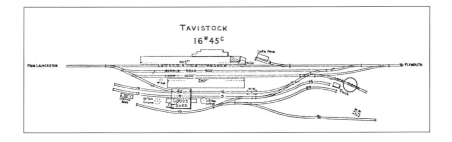

The north end of Tavistock South station. The signals for the northbound train are off, but the crew are still busy preparing the engine. The loading dock on the left was used for scrap metal consignments and other wagon load traffic.   *David Lawrence*

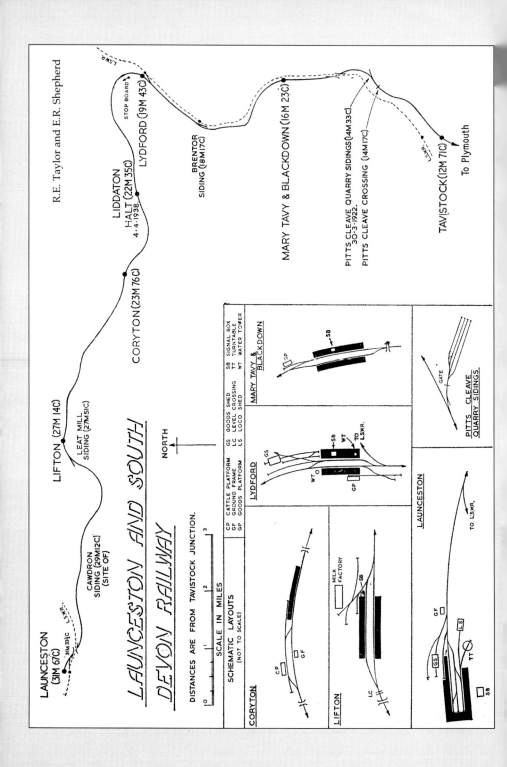

R.E. Taylor and E.R. Shepherd

LAUNCESTON AND SOUTH
DEVON RAILWAY

DISTANCES ARE FROM TAVISTOCK JUNCTION.

NORTH

SCALE IN MILES
0 1 2 3

LAUNCESTON (31M 67C)
3IM 33½C L.S.W.R.

LIFTON (27M 14C)
LEAT MILL SIDING (27M5IC)
CAWDRON SIDING (29M12C) (SITE OF)

CORYTON (23M 76C)

LIDDATON HALT (22M 35C) 4·4·1938.

LYDFORD (19M 43C)
STOP BOARD
L.SWR

BRENTOR SIDING (18M 17C)

MARY TAVY & BLACKDOWN (16M 23C)

PITTS CLEAVE QUARRY SIDINGS (14M 33C) 30·3·1922.
PITTS CLEAVE CROSSING (14M 17C)
L.S.W.R.

TAVISTOCK (12M 7IC)

To Plymouth

SCHEMATIC LAYOUTS
(NOT TO SCALE)

CP CATTLE PLATFORM   GS GOODS SHED   SB SIGNAL BOX
GF GROUND FRAME   LC LEVEL CROSSING   TT TURNTABLE
GP GOODS PLATFORM   LS LOCO SHED   WT WATER TOWER

MARY TAVY & BLACKDOWN
SB
GP

LYDFORD
GS
SB
WT
TO L.SWR.
WT O
GP

PITTS CLEAVE QUARRY SIDINGS
GATE

CORYTON
CP
GF

LIFTON
MILK FACTORY
SB
LC

LAUNCESTON
TO L.SWR.
GS
GF
LS
TT
SB

Chapter Eight

The Route Described
Tavistock to Launceston

Leaving Tavistock in a north-easterly direction, down trains crossed Plymouth road on a girder bridge and then proceeded along an embankment as they passed the 'Old Cemetery'. Beyond, the Great Western route soon converged with the London & South Western line, after which both lines maintained a parallel (albeit entirely separate) course for several miles.

Pitts Cleave Quarry Sidings

After about one and a half miles, down workings reached Pitts Cleave Quarry Sidings. Situated between the 14¼ and 14½ mileposts, the first siding here was brought into use on 30th March, 1922; a second was soon added, and then two more in June 1922. They were on the up side of the line, with a facing connection to down trains. The points were worked from a ground frame locked by key on the electric train staff for the Tavistock to Lydford section.

The quarry produced large quantities of roadstone for local authorities and ballast for the Great Western Railway engineering department. The roadstone was sent to Marsh Mills mainly in the firm's privately owned 20 ton hopper wagons. The ballast was forwarded in railway hoppers, often by engineering department special trains, but large quantities were also sent by ordinary freight services. The ballast was used mainly on the tracks in the Plymouth Division between Totnes and Cornwall.

There was an occupation level crossing leading to Pitts Cleave Quarry between Tavistock and Mary Tavy at 14 miles 17 chains, and this was equipped with a telephone so that the quarry operators could make contact with Tavistock South signal cabin when lorries or other heavy road vehicles crossed the running line.

When special trains called at the quarry sidings a shunter would travel out from Tavistock to assist the guard with shunting operations. On arrival at the quarry the guard or shunter was instructed to telephone Tavistock South box from the ground frame, and when the train was ready to leave the sidings, a further 'phone call was necessary so that the Tavistock South signalman could give his permission for the train to re-enter the main line.

Mary Tavy & Blackdown

Having passed the quarry sidings, northbound trains climbed steadily towards Mary Tavy & Blackdown. Situated at 16 miles 23 chains, this station was opened for passenger traffic on 1st July, 1865 and for goods traffic on 21st August, 1865. It was known as 'Mary Tavy' until 1907, when the words 'and Blackdown' were added to the station name.

Mary Tavy was originally a crossing place with up and down platforms, and

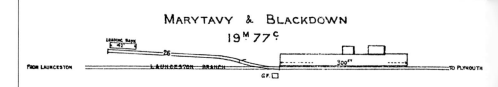

MARYTAVY & BLACKDOWN

19ᴹ 77ᶜ

LOADING BANK

26

FROM LAUNCESTON

LAUNCESTON BRANCH

300ᶠᵀ

GF. □

TO PLYMOUTH

Right: Mary Tavy and Blackdown signal box and station building as seen from the train on 20th August, 1954. The signal box had been out of use since the removal of the passing loop in 1890.

H.C. *Casserley*

Below: A general view of Mary Tavy and Blackdown looking towards Launceston.
Rural Publications: Nelson

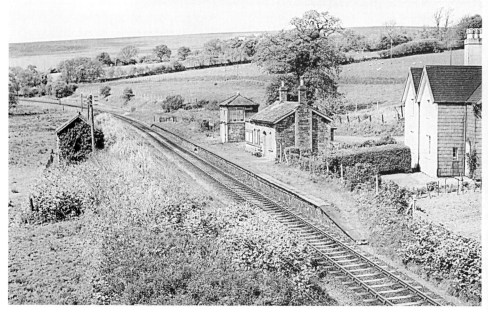

'45XX' class 2-6-2T No. 5569 seen near Brentor between Mary Tavy and Lydford, with the 2.05 pm Launceston to Plymouth train, 4th August, 1962.   The GWR's Launceston branch runs parallel to the LSWR's Devonport-Okehampton route at this point.   *Peter W. Gray*

'45XX' class 2-6-2T No. 5544 passes the ex-LSWR Brentor station with the 10.40 am Plymouth to Launceston service on 23rd September, 1961.   There was no Great Western station at Brentor, though a short goods siding was provided nearby at 18 miles 17 chains. Brentor LSWR station was opened on 2nd June, 1890.   *Peter W. Gray*

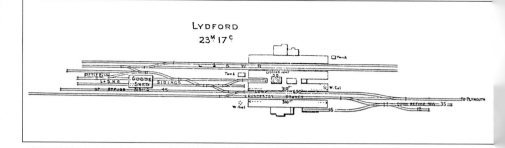

The approaches to Lydford station looking towards Plymouth. *Rural Publications: Nelson*

A view along the GWR platforms at Lydford station looking towards Launceston. The goods shed can be seen in the distance. The footbridge on the right links the GWR station to the Southern one. *Rural Publications: Nelson*

the crossing of trains was frequent between 1876 and 1890 when London & South Western trains travelled over the line between Lydford and Tavistock, *en route* to Devonport. The loop was taken out after this traffic ceased and the down side was closed; much later, the signal frame and signals were removed and a ground frame installed, this being locked by key on the train staff and worked by the guard of the freight train.

In the early 1900s the down platform was being used as a poultry run, but such utilitarian use of railway property was frowned on by authority, and the practice ceased.

The only staff employed was a booking constable in the early days; later by a station master of the lowest grade, who usually remained only a short while before going on to a more important station. In the early 1920s, for instance, the local station master was W.S. Medland, but in 1924 he left Mary Tavy to take up a new position at Lifton.

The surviving platform here was on the up side of the line; it had a length of 300 ft. The station building was a small, rectangular, gable-roofed structure incorporating the usual booking office, waiting room and toilet facilities. It was built of local stone with contrasting brick quoins, and its door and window apertures had pointed 'gothic' style arches; the architect was probably Peter J. Margary, who had been responsible for the construction of the Launceston & South Devon line.

Goods facilities consisted of a single dead-end siding on the up side, and this was entered by means of a connection that was facing to down trains. There was no goods shed or yard crane, though a 42 ft loading bank was available beside the solitary yard siding.

Mary Tavy became an unstaffed halt as from 11th August, 1941. The siding connection, ground frame and disc were removed on 14th December, 1948 and the halt was closed with effect from 31st December, 1962.

From Mary Tavy & Blackdown the single line continued north-westwards for about one mile, after which the route curved onto a northerly heading as it climbed towards Lydford on a series of rising gradients. In 1866 a short siding for the accommodation of local farmers and traders in the Brentor area was put in between Mary Tavy and Lydford stations at about 18 miles 17 chains.

Lydford

Lydford, the next station, was 19 miles 43 chains from Tavistock Junction and 23 miles 39 chains from Plymouth Millbay. It was known as 'Lidford' until 3rd June, 1897, when the modern spelling was adopted; the station was opened to passengers on 1st July, 1865 and to goods traffic on 21st August, 1865. It was closed to both on and from 31st December, 1962.

Lydford was the highest station on the line between Plymouth and Launceston, being 650 feet above mean sea level. It was a crossing station and had an up loop 567 feet long and a down loop of 595 feet.

The narrow gauge of the London & South Western Railway, which had opened to Okehampton on 3rd October, 1871, was extended to Lydford by 1874

Lydford station showing the signal box and island platform. To the left the LSWR station building can be seen, while a Southern parcels van occupies the short bay line. *David Lawrence*

'45XX' 2-6-2T No. 4555, now preserved, stands at Lydford on the 10.25 am Plymouth to Launceston train, 23rd June, 1962. *Peter W. Gray*

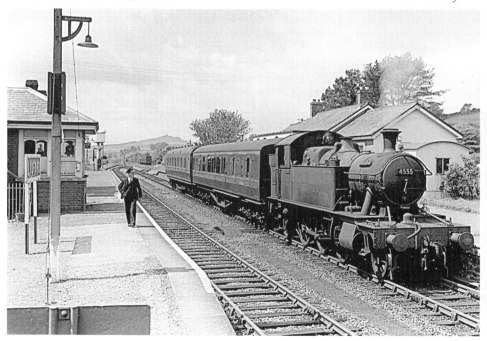

to a new station, built alongside the Launceston & South Devon station, which was opened to traffic on 12th October, 1874. Passengers for the South Devon line at that time had to change because of the break of gauge, and goods traffic had to be physically transferred from narrow to broad gauge wagons and vice versa. Much of the early traffic consisted of culm, and this traffic was transferred from wagon to wagon for as little as two pence per ton.

With the opening of the LSWR service to Devonport on 17th May, 1876 Lydford became the busiest station on the line between Marsh Mills and Launceston. This, situation continued until 2nd June, 1890 when the South Western commenced using the Plymouth, Devonport & South Western Junction company's line between Lydford and Plymouth.

The junction between the two companies at Lydford was not used after the latter date, but it remained in position until the latter part of 1895. The running powers exercised by the LSWR company over this section were enjoyed by section 14 of the Launceston & South Devon Railway Act of 1866 and remained in force until 31st December, 1947.

The junction line was equally divided in ownership, and by an agreement signed on 10th November, 1915 the GWR undertook to restore a connection on 28 days notice for emergency working.

Lydford was not, however, a joint station; although contiguous, the two stations were separate and each station originally had its own staff; supervision of the Great Western station was transferred to the LSWR company from 1st March, 1914, when the Great Western station master was withdrawn, but one GWR porter remained until at least 1917.

In architectural terms Lydford station exhibited a mixture of Great Western and London & South Western traditions. The main Great Western buildings were on the down side, and there was a smaller, waiting room block on the up platform. The main building was a gable-roofed structure with a centrally-placed main section and two projecting wings. The centre section was equipped with a platform canopy, and two squat chimney stacks extended from its roof.

The smaller building on the up platform was another gable-roofed building with gothic-style window and door openings; from its general appearance, this structure had probably originated as the main building when the railway was first opened in 1865. However, when the London & South Western platforms were constructed on the eastern side of the Great Western line the GWR station was re-orientated - the original Launceston & South Devon station building being down-graded to subsidiary status, while a new range of buildings was erected on the west (i.e. down) side of the GWR line.

On 8th January, 1917 the Great Western signal box at milepost 19¼ at the Plymouth end of the down platform, and the London & South Western signal box at the Okehampton end of the down platform, were closed, and a new box on the centre platform, manned by LSWR signalmen was brought into use the same day. This box had two frames at opposite ends of the operating floor, and it straddled the agreed boundary between the stations, the Great Western frame being on GWR property. Although not a joint station, the staff then employed at Lydford wore uniforms which bore the insignia of the Great Western and London & South Western companies.

'45XX' class 2-6-2T No. 4591 leaves Lydford on the 10.40 am Plymouth-Launceston service on 15th April, 1961.   *Peter W. Gray*

'45XX' class 2-6-2T No. 5544 arrives at Liddaton Halt on the 12.14 pm Plymouth-Launceston working on 3rd June, 1962.   *Peter W. Gray*

Lydford's goods facilities were concentrated on the up side of the line to the north of the passenger platforms, on a restricted site between the Great Western and LSWR lines.   Three dead-end sidings were provided, together with a system of connecting loops and spurs; access from the GWR side of the station was arranged by means of a trailing connection from the up main line, while LSWR goods trains could reverse into the yard via a similar connection from the down London & South Western line.

A large, gable-roofed goods shed occupied a strategic position near the centre of the goods yard, and it is interesting to note that this building was at one time used as a transfer shed between the broad and narrow gauges of the GWR and the LSWR companies.

There were, in addition to the goods sidings, up and down refuge lines with sufficient room for 43 goods vehicles in the up siding and 26 wagons on the down side.   Further sidings were installed at Lydford in connection with wartime traffic in 1943.

Other work carried out at Lydford during World War II included the provision of an emergency connection between the GWR and Southern lines some 97 yards on the Brentor side of the signal box. This connection was laid in May 1943 and brought into use as from 21st June, 1943. It was removed in November 1947.

Like other country stations, Lydford was rationalised in the 1960s, the up running siding, down loop and GWR down sidings being taken out of use in May 1963 and removed in 1965. The electric train tokens at Lydford, Lifton and Launceston were removed in September 1964, after which 'one engine in steam' working was introduced in connection with the remaining freight services to Launceston.

The gradient between Tavistock and Lydford rose for about six miles with a maximum of 1 in 63 over varying lengths. Assisting engines for goods trains were placed behind down trains at Tavistock station and pushed thence to Lydford, uncoupled. If they had to go beyond Lydford, they had to be placed in front of the trains at that station. Up freight trains were assisted from the rear between Lifton and Lydford.

Between Lydford and Coryton there was a falling gradient of 1 in 55 for a distance of 44 chains, and down trains had to stop at a stop board situated at 19 miles 45 chains. The line also fell towards Mary Tavy, and all freight trains (up or down) upon arrival at Lydford, had to be placed in the refuge siding clear of the main line, before any shunting was commenced.

Liddaton Halt

After Lydford, down workings were able to coast downhill for several miles, Lydford station being the summit of the Launceston & South Devon section. Lydford also marked the spot at which the London & South Western line parted company with the GWR branch, and having diverged sharply leftwards, and away from the LSWR main line, the Great Western route continued due west through the Lyd valley.

Situated at 22 miles 35 chains (26 miles 9 chains from Millbay), Liddaton Halt

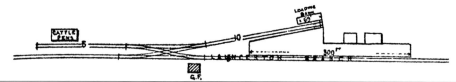

'45XX' class 2-6-2T No. 4555 arrives at Coryton with a train from Launceston, 23rd June, 1962.
R.C. Riley

Coryton station looking towards Plymouth.   *Rural Publications: Nelson*

was not opened until 4th April, 1938. It served a small community of scattered farms and cottages, and enabled local people to travel to Launceston or Tavistock for shopping expeditions or visits to the weekly markets.

The halt was of simple, wooden construction, with oil lamps and a small timber shelter; for administrative purposes it was supervised from nearby Coryton station. Up trains were faced with a 1 in 55 gradient at this point. The halt was closed on and from 31st December, 1962, when passenger services were withdrawn from the Launceston branch.

Coryton

From Liddaton Halt the single line headed due west and, dropping at 1 in 55, the railway followed a stretch of embankments as it neared the next station at Coryton, some 23 miles 76 chains from Tavistock Junction. An original station opened on 1st July, 1865, Coryton was one of the smaller intermediate stopping places. It had just one platform, on the up side of the line, and the stone station building was similar to those at Mary Tavy and Lydford; the platform was 300 ft long, and its surface was partially paved with stone slabs.

Coryton's goods facilities consisted of a single goods siding which, until the 1930s, had been linked to the running line by a 'scissors' crossover; later, however, this arrangement was altered, and in BR days the siding was connected to the main line by conventional trailing and facing crossovers. At its eastern end, the goods siding terminated in a loading dock, while at its western end the line served a cattle loading pen. Access to the goods yard was controlled by a ground frame.

Other facilities at Coryton included a small platelayers' hut and a standard Great Western corrugated iron goods lock-up - the latter building being sited on the platform, to the west of the station building. No signal box was provided, and the station was not a block post.

Although Coryton was one of the smallest stations *en route* to Launceston it had, in earlier years at least, been considered important enough to have its own station master - this position being filled, during the early 1920s, by Mr J.K. Endacott, who subsequently moved to Burngullow on the Cornish main line.

In the 19th century the station had dealt with large quantities of manganese traffic, and in 1868-69 the tonnage loaded was 900 tons; by 1872 this figure had reached 4,000 tons per annum. The station served a quiet rural area, and its general freight traffic remained fairly stable over a period of 35 years up to 1939. It was reduced to unstaffed halt and public siding status on 14th September, 1959; the ground frame and siding connections were taken out of use on 31st March, 1965.

Coryton itself was a small village, about one mile east from the station; it had a Perpendicular church that had been heavily restored in Victorian times. (One of the tombstones commemorated Gabriel Wood 'who had sonns three but not one good'!) Coryton station also served the neighbouring village of Lew Trenchard, some two miles to the north of the railway. Lew Trenchard House had been the home of the Reverend Sabine Baring-Gould (1834-1924), the famous Devonshire hymn-writer and local historian, whose works included *Songs of the*

The north end of Coryton station showing the goods facilities. No. 4570 stands at the platform with the 3.05 pm Plymouth to Launceston train, 4th August, 1962. *Peter W. Gray*

Lifton station from the north in the early years of this century. *Lens of Sutton*

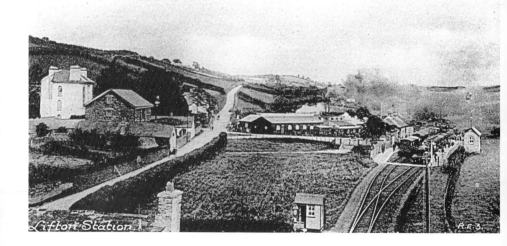

West (a collection of local folk songs) and the Anglican hymns *Through the Night of Doubt and Sorrow, Now the Day is Over* and *Onward Christian Soldiers*. (Sadly for local historians, the latter hymn was written not in Devon, but in Yorkshire.)

Lifton

Leaving Coryton, down trains passed beneath a road overbridge and, with the River Lyd flowing more or less parallel to the south, the route dropped towards Launceston on a series of falling gradients - Lifton, the next stop, being approached on a 1 in 140 descent. This station, opened on 1st July, 1865 for passengers and on 21st August, 1865 for goods traffic, was 27 miles 14 chains from Tavistock Junction and 30 miles 68 chains from Plymouth Millbay.

A two platform crossing station, Lifton had up and down platforms, the main station buildings and goods yard being on the up side of the line. The station building was a substantially-built stone structure with a hipped, slated roof. Internally, it contained the usual waiting room and booking office.

Lifton's goods yard was rebuilt in 1870 at a cost of £150, and in 1894 a private siding was provided for Bryley's corn mills. Later, a large rail-served dairy was erected, and this brought much extra traffic to the station - especially in BR days, when milk was despatched in bulk tank wagons.

The goods yard was situated on the up side, access from the up loop being arranged by means of a trailing connection. There were, in all, three short sidings in the goods yard proper. The longest siding ended in a 40 ft loading dock behind the up platform, and this siding had a capacity of 12 short wheelbase wagons. The other two sidings were even shorter, with a capacity of four and five wagons respectively. Additionally, Bryley's mill siding formed a sort of 'kick back' spur from the main goods yard - entry to this facility being obtained only by means of a reverse shunt from the yard sidings; the corn mill siding could hold up to 15 wagons.

Interestingly, the dairy at Lifton was built on land leased from the GWR under an agreement signed in 1917 between the railway and the Ambrosia company, and for this reason no private siding arrangements were needed - the dairy being conveniently sited beside the outermost yard siding. The mill siding, in contrast, was a conventional private siding, provided under an agreement between the GWR and R. Bryley that dated from 1893. A new agreement, made between the railway company and the Lifton Milling Company, was signed in October 1922.

There was no goods shed, as such, at Lifton, though a small stone-built lockup was provided on the up platform for small parcels, packages and general merchandise traffic. A six-ton yard crane had evidently been installed at the station by 1938, this facility being listed in the 1938 Railway Clearing House *Handbook of Stations*, together with the usual range of cattle pens and loading docks.

Lifton signal box was a diminutive, single-storey cabin. Situated on the up platform, it measured around 15 ft x 7 ft at ground level, and contained a 17-lever frame. There were, however, no train staff instruments in the box, the train staff being kept in the nearby booking office.

'45XX' class 2-6-2T No. 5541, arrives at Lifton on a train for Launceston. The dairy can be seen behind the up platform.   *Rural Publications: Nelson*

A view along the platforms at Lifton looking towards Launceston. Beyond the level crossing gates the arch which carried a narrow gauge line to Tinhay Quarry can be clearly seen.

Rural Publications: Nelson

A level crossing at the west end of the station was opened and closed manually; the gates were locked by a key arrangement and by a lever in a small ground frame hut - the latter being released by lever No. 10 in the signal box.

Other facilities at Lifton included a small waiting shelter on the down platform, a corrugated iron lamp hut on the up platform, a station house which was completed in November 1928, an up loop 510 feet long, and a down loop 604 feet long. The signal box was reduced to ground frame status, and all signals except the up and down distants and the down home were removed in September 1964.

Lifton was an important station serving a wide agricultural district, and it dealt with a large tonnage of grain traffic for Lifton Mills. In addition to the milk tank traffic referred to above, large quantities of dried milk were forwarded by passenger train.

Lifton lost its passenger and goods services in December 1962, but the line between Lifton and Lydford was retained to enable the Lifton milk traffic to be worked under special arrangements to Lydford and thence to Plymouth by the former Southern Railway, for conveyance thence by the 5.50 pm milk train from Penzance to Kensington Olympia. This arrangement continued until 28th February, 1966, when the goods line to the milk factory was finally closed.

Leaving Lifton, down trains rumbled over the gated level crossing at the west end of the station. Continuing westwards, the line dropped towards its destination on a 1 in 192 falling gradient, which soon eased to 1 in 440, and then 1 in 270. With the River Lyd only a short distance away, trains passed the tiny hamlet of Leat, at which point a private siding branched out on the north side of the line to serve Leat corn mills.

Leat siding was connected to the main line by a trailing connection in the up direction at 27 miles 51 chains, which was worked from a ground frame locked by an Annett's Key. Guards who had to work at the siding were especially instructed to ensure that all trucks were well inside the catch points and firmly secured. Up freight trains only were permitted to call at the siding, which is not shown on the early Ordnance Survey maps, but which appears in the time table for 1876. The ground frame and the siding connection were removed on 21st November, 1943.

Running now on favourable gradients, the line undulated westwards towards Launceston, the final three miles being on gently rising inclinations of 1 in 218, 1 in 2033 and 1 in 122, followed - at the very end of the journey - by a stretch of 1 in 146.

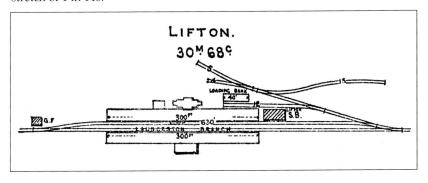

'45XX' class 2-6-2T No. 4591 is seen near Launceston at the head of the 12.10 pm Plymouth-Launceston service on 17th September, 1953.   *T.G. Wassall*

The World War II-built link between the GWR and SR at Launceston *c.* 1962. The original GWR line is on the right. From 1952 all Western Region passenger trains used the former LSWR station.   *L. Crosier*

Launceston

At 29 miles 12 chains, trains passed the site of Cawdron (or Lifton) Quarry siding, which had been ordered to be made by the Board of Trade on 19th September, 1865 after an application had been received from the quarry owner, Mr A.W. Arundell. It was out of use by 1894.

Crossing the River Tamar on a small bridge, the line passed beneath the London & South Western line from Halwill Junction to Launceston and Padstow, which had been opened through to Launceston on 21st July, 1886. The rival lines then continued westwards along a parallel course, with the LSWR running to the south of the Great Western branch.

At Launceston North Junction the World War II emergency link between the two systems diverged to the left. The junction was at 31 miles 33½ chains, and was a single connecting line, facing to down trains. It was opened with a new east ground frame on the up side as an engineering department siding, on 6th April, 1943, and was used for War emergency traffic as from 22nd September, of that year. The line was wholly Southern Railway property.

With their destination now in sight, trains slowed for the final approach to Launceston, and with sidings visible on both sides of the running line, the 35 mile 38 chain journey from Plymouth came to an end in a classic Great Western country branch terminus.

This was the northern extremity of the Launceston & South Devon Railway, the distance from Tavistock Junction being 31 miles 64½ chains to the centre of the platform, though the line extended to 31 miles 67 chains at the buffer stops. The suffix 'North' was added to the station name on 18th June, 1951. It had its first train on 1st June, 1865 when the formal opening of the line took place, but it was not until 1st July, 1865 that the line was opened to passengers. Goods traffic was dealt with from 21st August, 1865. The station was closed to passenger traffic on 30th June, 1952, when passenger trains were diverted to and from the Southern Railway via the World War II junction line.

The goods depot was reduced to siding status under the supervision of the Southern Region staff as from 31st December, 1962, and was finally closed on 28th February, 1966.

The station comprised a 350 ft passenger platform with passenger and goods run-round loops, a goods shed, engine shed, water crane and a 45 ft turntable. There was good siding accommodation for the large mineral and agricultural traffic dealt with. Livestock traffic was heavy, especially on Tuesdays, when the weekly cattle market was held and a special cattle train run. Although in many ways a conventional GWR branch terminus, Launceston had one unusual (though by no means unique) feature. This peculiarity concerned the way in which the goods yard was entered from the run-round loop, necessitating a flat crossing of the running line. This somewhat complex arrangement was simplified around 1930, when a new connection, facing to down trains, was installed on the running line. (It is difficult to see what purpose the original layout could have served - other than the avoidance of a facing connection on the main running line.)

Launceston's Great Western station buildings were of stone construction, the main building material being coursed stonework. The window and door

Two early postcard views of the two stations at Launceston. *Above*: the GWR lines are in the foreground. *Lower*: the LSWR station is in the foreground with the GWR station and goods shed beyond it.   *Lens of Sutton/Geof Sheppard Collection*

St. Stephens from Launceston.

Launceston GWR station; by the time this photograph was taken the GWR station was being used for goods traffic only.   *Lens of Sutton*

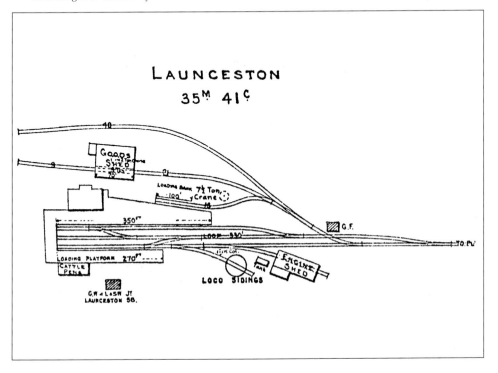

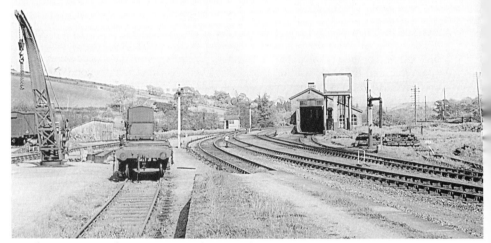

The GWR engine shed viewed from the end of the Great Western platforms at Launceston.

Rural Publications: Nelson

'45XX' class 2-6-2T No. 5541 is seen on the approaches to the former LSWR station. In the background is the ex-GWR engine shed, 2nd May, 1961. *R.C. Riley*

openings had semi-circular, Italianate-style arches, and the building was covered by a low-pitched gable roof. There were protecting canopies at both the front and rear - the front (platform) canopy being a full length structure supported by a row of seven, centrally-placed timber uprights.

Close examination of the building suggested that, as first designed, it had been the intention to erect an overall train shed. The platform-facing facade was entirely flat, and the front wall of the building was continued up, beyond the gutter level, to form a continuous parapet that rose several feet above the canopy; this substantial front wall was clearly designed to form one side of a train shed - though, as we have seen, the South Devon Railway decided not to cover the station when the matter was raised during the early 1870s.

Launceston's Great Western goods shed was a typical broad gauge-style structure, similar sheds being found throughout the GWR system. A relatively large, stone-built structure, the goods shed featured large arched openings through which railway vehicles could enter the building for loading or unloading purposes. Internally, the shed contained a 75 ft loading platform and a two ton hand crane to facilitate the transfer of heavy loads between road and rail vehicles. Sliding doors protected the entrances, and the interior was lit by arched windows which echoed those on the neighbouring station building.

The goods yard contained two long sidings, one of which passed through the goods shed while the other ran along the northern edge of the yard; the latter siding could hold up to 40 short-wheelbase goods vehicles. A much shorter siding diverged from the goods shed line to serve an end-loading dock, and there was, in addition, a 270 ft goods loading platform on the south side of the passenger station - the latter facility being equipped with cattle loading pens for livestock traffic.

The engine shed, which was reached by a short spur from the passenger station, was a stone building measuring approximately 100 ft x 22 ft at ground level. The shed was lit by arched windows along each side, and a small office-cum mess room was provided in a 35 ft x 15 ft lean-to extension on the south side of the main shed building.

The shed was flanked by a group of ancillary structures including a small coaling stage, a sand furnace and a stilted water tank. The water tank incorporated a water column with a rotating boom from which the branch locomotives could replenish their tanks.

Launceston shed was a sub-shed of Plymouth (Laira), and its allocation at the time of nationalisation was '45XX' class 2-6-2T No. 4524.

Launceston station was well sited in relation to both the LSWR station (which was literally 'next door') and the town, and visitors arriving by rail were brought within a short distance of the town centre. The main tourist attractions here included the parish church and the famous castle - the latter being sited in a prominent position on the south-eastern side of the town.

The castle, which was damaged during the civil war of 1642-46, was said to have been much out of repair by 1650 and although parts of the Medieval building remained in use as a prison for many years, the castle grounds were subsequently landscaped to form an attractive public park. In World War II the ruined fortress was once again used for military purpose when the Air Ministry erected hutted accommodation in the bailey, but with the return of peace Launceston Castle passed

The two stations at Launceston.

Reproduced from the 6", 1938 Ordnance Survey Map

into the guardianship of the Ministry of Works. As such, the remaining buildings enjoyed protected status as an Ancient Monument; the site is now administered by English Heritage, who have established a small museum* within the castle grounds.

The Great Western Railway served a predominantly rural area with few heavy industries, and for this reason the company was understandably keen to promote tourism as a means of increasing revenue from passenger traffic. In furtherance of this aim the Great Western produced an attractive range of guidebooks and scholarly works - among the latter being a substantial study by Charles Oman entitled *Castles* (1926). This publication was sold at station booking offices as well as in retail outlets, and it included a useful description of Launceston Castle, together with details of Pendennis, St Mawes, Restormal, Totnes and other local fortresses.

In another attempt to foster the links between railways, tourism and what would today be called the Heritage industry, the GWR also named many of its locomotives after historic buildings - one of these being 'Castle' class 4-6-0 No. 5000 *Launceston Castle*.

Reverting to strictly railway matters, it would be appropriate to make at least some mention of the London & South Western Railway station, which was situated immediately to the south of the GWR station, and became Launceston's only passenger station in June 1952.

The South Western station was a two-platform stopping place with up and down platforms. A long headshunt extended eastwards from the down loop line and this gave access to the goods yard and engine shed sidings. The main station building was on the down platform and there was a much smaller waiting room on the up side. Both buildings were of stone construction, the main block being a 'hall-and-cross wings' design with a central portion and prominent cross wings. The LSWR station was also fully equipped with the usual range of cattle pens, loading docks and goods storage facilities.

Before finally leaving Launceston it is worth recalling that, if earlier plans had come to fruition, the Great Western branch would have been extended beyond its existing terminus to join the Bude Canal in the Parish of Werrington.

The Bude Canal & Launceston Junction Railway Company obtained its Act (28 & 29 Vic. cap. 263) on 5th July, 1865. Capital of £20,000 in shares and £6,000 in loans was authorised to pay for this 2¾ mile line, and the Engineer was J.F.W. Featherstonhauge. It was assumed that, when completed, the Bude Canal & Launceston Junction Railway would be worked by the Launceston & South Devon company, but at a time when there was much talk of a standard gauge link to Launceston provision was also made for a possible future link to any 4 ft 8½ in. gauge line.

The project was primarily a local scheme, and its leading supporters included Daniel Shilson of Launceston, John Ching of Launceston and George A. Hillier of London. Sadly, the Bude Canal & Launceston Junction project was not implemented - the promoters having failed to raise sufficient capital during a period of financial crisis. On the other hand, the threat of such a line being built seems to have worried the Bude Canal proprietors, and perhaps for this reason they lowered the tolls on the Druxton branch of the canal, thereby pleasing local traders (but hurting the pockets of their own shareholders!).

* Now closed as a result of staffing cuts.

A 1930s view at Launceston, with the former LSWR platforms in the foreground and a GWR train in the distance. Note the Joint signal box.
Lens of Sutton

A view of the eastern end of the ex-LSWR station on 2nd March, 1954. By this time the passenger trains on the Launceston branch were using this station as their terminus. One of R.E.V. Maunsell's 'N' class 2-6-0s No. 31842 is seen leaving with the 2.02 pm train for Waterloo, while in the platform '45XX' class No. 4530 waits to take the 2.10 pm to Plymouth.
Peter W. Gray

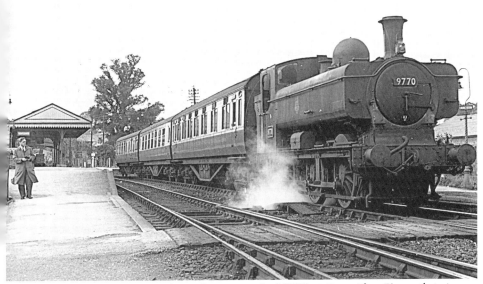

'57XX' class 0-6-0PT No. 9770 leaves Launceston (ex-LSWR) station with a Plymouth train, August 1953.   *Real Photographs*

'45XX' class 2-6-2T No. 4583 is seen taking water at Launceston having just arrived with a train from Plymouth on 12th July, 1956.   *Frank Hornby*

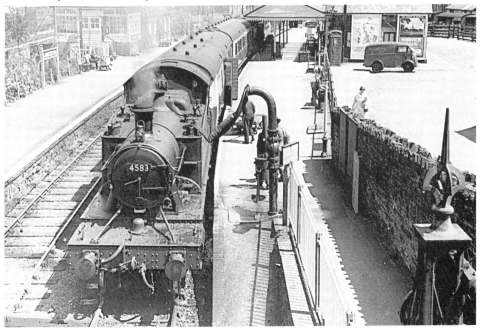

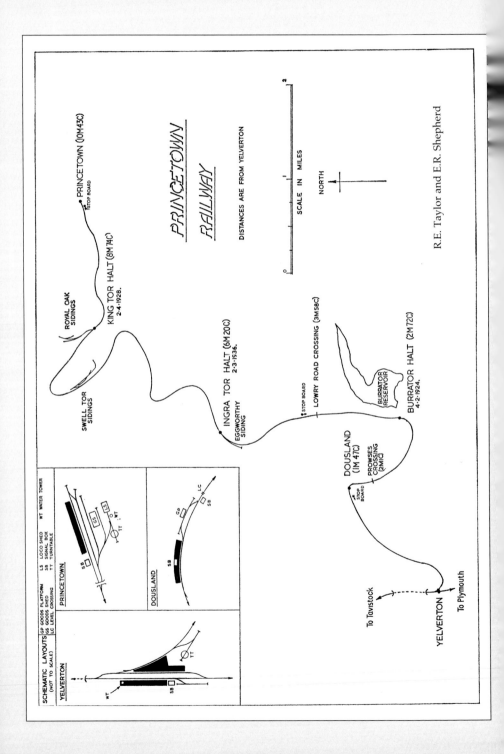

PRINCETOWN RAILWAY

DISTANCES ARE FROM YELVERTON

SCALE IN MILES

NORTH

R.E. Taylor and E.R. Shepherd

PRINCETOWN (10M 43C)
STOP BOARD

KING TOR HALT (8M 74C)
2·4·1928.

ROYAL OAK
SIDINGS

SWELL TOR
SIDINGS

INGRA TOR HALT (6M 20C)
2·3·1936.

EGGWORTHY
SIDING

STOP BOARD

LOWRY ROAD CROSSING (3M 58C)

BURRATOR
RESERVOIR

BURRATOR HALT (2M 72C)
4·2·1924.

DOUSLAND
(1M 47C)

PROWSES
CROSSING
(2MILE)

STOP
BOARD

To Tavistock

YELVERTON

To Plymouth

SCHEMATIC LAYOUTS
(NOT TO SCALE)

GP GOODS PLATFORM   LS LOCO SHED   WT WATER TOWER
GS GOODS SHED   SB SIGNAL BOX
LC LEVEL CROSSING   TT TURNTABLE

PRINCETOWN

SB
GS
LS
TT
WT

DOUSLAND

SB
GP
LC
SB

YELVERTON

WT
SB
TT

Chapter Nine

The Princetown Railway

It is probably true that but for the life and ambitions of Thomas Tyrwhitt there would have been no Princetown, no Dartmoor Prison, no Plymouth & Dartmoor Railway and no Princetown Railway.

Thomas Tyrwhitt, born on 12th August, 1762, came to Dartmoor as a wealthy young man in 1785 and became so interested in experiments then being carried out that he embarked upon an ambitious scheme to reclaim large portions of the Forest of Dartmoor. He built roads, enclosed land, commenced afforestation and built for himself a large house which he named Tor Royal, near the Prince Hall estate, and which he completed in 1798.

He was Member of Parliament for Okehampton from 1796-1802, and was also Member for Plymouth between 1806-12. During the Napoleonic War he persuaded the Government to build a Prison of War on Dartmoor for French prisoners, the foundation of which he laid on 20th March, 1806. The building was completed in 1809 at a cost of £127,000 and for the next seven years it was used, first by French prisoners from 1809-14, then by American prisoners from 1813-15, and again by the French from 1815-16. The village of Princetown grew up around the prison which soon had a church, built by the French and fitted out by American prisoners.

In 1812, Tyrwhitt resigned as Member of Parliament and became knighted upon being appointed Gentleman Usher of the Black Rod. He also became private secretary to, and a close friend of, the Prince of Wales.

After peace treaties had been signed with the French and with the Americans Dartmoor prison became empty and was closed, the town was deserted with grass-grown streets, closed shops, houses and church. After nine years in London, Sir Thomas returned to Dartmoor and renewed his activities on behalf of the people, securing for the town the privilege of holding a fair and a market.

The great need of the district was transport with Plymouth, which in his own words, would 'reduce the price of provisions, find employment and give support to a great number of orphan and pauper children and employment for the industrious poor' who, in pursuance of his scheme for developing, cultivating and repopulating the district, would be brought from the Metropolis to Dartmoor, housed in the prison buildings, receive religious instruction and then be trained in the cultivation and spinning of flax and in re-claiming waste land for more general cultivation. In the event, the orphans, paupers and 'industrious poor' were not evacuated to Dartmoor and this part of Sir Thomas' scheme was abandoned in 1822.

The Plymouth & Dartmoor Railway

In the meantime, the proposal for a railway from Plymouth to Princetown took shape. Sir Thomas put forward his proposals on 3rd November, 1818 to the Plymouth Chamber of Commerce. The idea was readily accepted and plans were deposited with the Clerk of the Peace for the County of Devon on 30th November, 1818, enabling a Bill to be presented to Parliament in the 1819 session; this became a law on 2nd July, 1819. It incorporated the Plymouth & Dartmoor Railway Company and authorised the making of a line about 24½ miles in length, commencing at a point near Laira on the eastern side of Plymouth, and running thence to Jump via Leigham and Fursdon, on to Clearbrook, Yelverton Common, Dousland and Yennadon Down to the foot of Peek Hilk and thence to Ingra Tor, around Swell Tor to King Tor and on to Princetown. The estimated cost of making this line was £27,783; powers were also obtained to raise an additional £5,000.

Further Acts were obtained on 8th July, 1820 for an extension to Sutton Pool (Plymouth) at a cost of £7,200 and on 2nd July, 1821 for deviations and a tunnel at Leigham at a cost of £5,000, making a total estimated cost of £39,983 for the whole line, which was to prove hopelessly inadequate.

The first rail was laid by Sir Thomas on 12th August, 1819, and the first section between Crabtree (Laira) and King Tor, the temporary terminus (approximately 23 miles), was completed by 26th September, 1823.

Sir Thomas, in his speech at the opening ceremony, said that the railway:

Would gratify the lover of the country, reward the capitalists, promote the agricultural, mechanical and commercial arts, encourage home settlement, add a large quantity of improved land, strength and population to the kingdom, and finally expand into a boundless field of speculation, ever calling for fresh capital and ever yielding new incentives to industrious emulation, local prosperity and public improvement.

The Sutton Harbour section of the line was completed by December 1825, and the King Tor to Princetown portion was opened by December 1826; a line connecting with the Cann Quarry Canal (opened on 20th November, 1829) was converted to a through line to the Quarry by 1834, and a further branch line from the Cann Quarry branch was constructed from Marsh Mills to Plympton and opened in the same year. All of these lines, which were worked by horses, were built to a gauge of 4 ft 6 in.

Sir Thomas died in 1833 and did not see the fulfilment of his life's ambition.

By 1835 the line was dealing with a large quantity of granite from the Moor, slate stone from Cann Quarry and china clay from Plympton, and to all outward appearances was fulfilling its declared purpose, but its finances were in a sorry state. The total cost of the line was 'about £66,000'. The public had subscribed £37,000 and the Exchequer had supplied another £28,000, but Messrs Johnson Brothers who worked the granite quarries had so dominated the position that the line over Dartmoor was virtually their private railway. They had secured for themselves the very low rate of 2s. 6d. per ton for the transport of granite from the Moor to Plymouth, irrespective of distance, and, they held such power that even this low rate was later reduced to the ridiculous figure of one shilling a ton.

The production of granite from the quarries at Ingra Tor, Swell Tor and Foggintor continued to increase between 1830-40 when upwards of 600 men were often employed. Later, quarrying declined and it was not until the prison was converted and reopened as a convict establishment on 21st November, 1850 that prosperity returned to Princetown.

But changes were already on the way. In 1847 the South Devon Railway Company, to secure their line of approach to Plymouth, purchased from the Plymouth & Dartmoor Railway that section of their line between Plympton and Marsh Mills. By 1851 they had purchased from Johnson Brothers (the ostensible owners) the line between Crabtree and Sutton Pool, which they reconstructed to a mixed gauge of 4 ft 6 in. and 7 ft 0¼ in.

On 5th July, 1852 the South Devon & Tavistock promoters agreed with Lord Morley on the construction of a new branch line to the Lee Moor clayworks as part of their scheme for a line to Tavistock. The branch line was to be an extension of the lower end of the Plymouth & Dartmoor Railway and part of the Cann Quarry branch (see *The Plymouth & Dartmoor Railway*, by H.G. Kendall for further details).

In 1865 the Plymouth & Dartmoor company was reconstituted by Act dated 3rd May, 1865, which confirmed the position of Johnson Brothers, and authorised the creation of preference shares worth £75,000, all in favour of William Johnson. On 19th April, 1869 steam locomotion was introduced on the broad gauge of the Sutton Harbour line and by 1869-70 matters had so improved that the company was able to declare a maiden dividend of 5s. per £100 share!

The Princetown Railway

But to return to the Princetown end of the line. As mentioned above, the prospectus of the South Devon & Tavistock Railway, issued on 5th July, provided, *inter alia*, that 'the line will be so arranged that if found desirable, it may be formed to Government establishments at Princetown, or the existing railway modified for that purpose.' This question was raised at the half-yearly meeting of the Tavistock company held on 29th August, 1857, but, although the matter was favourably received, it was decided that nothing could be done at that stage apart from recommending it to the Directors for consideration. It was to be another twenty-five years before the time was ripe for the suggested development.

At the half-yearly meeting on 6th March, 1877 of the Great Western Railway (now in possession of the South Devon & Tavistock line), the matter of a proposed line from Princetown, Dartmoor, to the Plymouth & Tavistock Railway, a little more than seven miles long', was discussed and it was agreed that the Great Western would take powers to make the line if all land-owners would come forward liberally - as one had already done - and if the Government gave assistance by making the first three miles from Princetown by convict labour. If this were done the Great Western would make the rest of the line at a cost of £52,000. This was followed by a meeting at Princetown held on 14th March, 1877 at the Duchy Hotel, presided over by Captain Hume, Deputy Governor of the Prison, to consider an approach to the Great Western Railway Company for a line to Princetown.

Later, however, the Great Western withdrew their scheme for a branch line to Princetown in favour of a proposal made by the Plymouth & Dartmoor company that they should sell their railway from Princetown to a point at

Yelverton in the parish of Buckland Monachorum, including the rails, chairs and sleepers, for a consideration of 2,200 'C' shares of £10 each, fully paid up, of a new company to be called the Princetown Railway Company.

Plans were deposited at 10.45 am on 30th November, 1877 for a line 10 miles 2 furlongs 2.8 chains long, with a rising gradient, over the whole distance except for a short section from 3 miles 6½ furlongs to 4 miles 2 furlongs where the gradient was 1 in 51 falling toward Princetown. The starting point was at a junction near the north end of Yelverton Siding, and south of the tunnel under Roborough Down (Elfordtown to Harrowbeer). Strangely enough, the name of the engineer was not given.

The Bill, which confirmed a scheduled memorandum of agreement dated 16th July, 1878 between the promoters and the Plymouth & Dartmoor company, received the Royal Assent on 13th August, 1878. The estimated cost of construction was £57,147.

The Great Western Railway had power to subscribe up to £30,000, which they did by taking 4 per cent 'A' preference stock, and the Plymouth & Dartmoor company, £22,000, this being the purchase price agreed, which they held in 'C' shares of £10 each fully paid up in the new company. The Great Western had power to appoint four Directors and the Plymouth & Dartmoor company three.

By an agreement dated 18th January, 1883, the line was to be worked in perpetuity by the Great Western company upon payment of a percentage of the gross receipts, but not to exceed 70 per cent. This was, in fact, paid throughout the working period up to 31st December, 1921, when the line was absorbed into the Great Western as from 1st January, 1922 by the Railway Act of 19th August, 1921 and the Great Western Railway (Western Group) Preliminary Absorption Scheme, No. 1, 19th May, 1922.

There were no special celebrations to mark the opening of the line which took place on 11th August, 1883. A brief announcement in the *Western Daily Mercury* of that date stated that the Great Western would no doubt be 'hoping to convey as many passengers from the Three Towns as have the leisure and desire, to Dartmoor. There are not to be any Sunday trains but there will be four trains every week day between Horrabridge and Princetown.'

The Princetown Railway was laid to the standard gauge but its trains ran over the mixed gauge between the junction to the north of Yelverton Siding and Horrabridge (which had been laid in for London & South Western trains to travel to and from Lidford and Plymouth) up to 1st May, 1885 when a passenger station was opened at Yelverton, which then became a junction station.

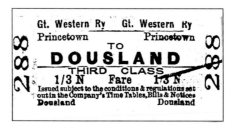

Ordinary GWR single ticket (green).   *John M. Strange Collection*

The Route of the Princetown Branch

At Yelverton the branch platform was on a curve which continued on an embankment for about a mile on a rising gradient of 1 in 40. After the curve the line went through a cutting on to the natural ground following the old Dartmoor Railway with the main Plymouth to Exeter road on the left, before arriving at Dousland station, 1 mile 47 chains from Yelverton.

From Dousland, with its level crossing, the line passed over another crossing, Prowse's, at 2 miles 1 chain and then made a wide sweep around Yennadon Down, with its fine view of the valley of the Meavy, to Burrator Halt.

Opened on 4th February, 1924, Burrator Halt was situated at 2 miles 72 chains from Yelverton and 1 mile 25 chains from Dousland. The Halt was on an embankment which gave a fine view of Burrator reservoir, Plymouth's main water supply, an artificial lake about 11 miles long which harmonised well with the general scene, being surrounded by woods and plantations, and overlooked by Sheeps Tor which rose to 844 ft behind the nearby village of that name.

The halt was much used from the date of opening by Plymouth Corporation workmen who travelled daily to and from Plymouth to work on raising the reservoir dam.

From Burrator Halt the line was taken through a short cutting before coming to the western side of Peek Hill with Lether Tor and Sharpitor (1,214 ft) prominent. Passing Lowry Road level crossing, at 3 miles 58 chains the line was on a downhill gradient of 1 in 41 for a distance of half a mile; this was the only piece of downhill between Yelverton and Princetown.

From the 4½ milepost to Princetown, a distance of 6¼ miles, the line continuously rose with sharp curves, passed Ingra Tor Halt, at 6 miles 20 chains, opened 2nd March, 1936, with its unusual warning notice to passengers to keep dogs on the lead because of the presence of snakes on the Moor. Then came Swell Tor Siding at 7 miles 63 chains and King Tor Halt, opened on 2nd April, 1928, 8 miles 74 chains from Yelverton. From King Tor Halt to Princetown, a distance of 1 mile 69 chains the gradient was 1 in 47.

King Tor itself, rises to 1,314 feet and the loop around it, about 2½ miles long, was so narrow that a person could meet a train at the beginning of the loop, walk across the neck of the quarries and arrive at the northern end of the Tor before the train reached that point! The three halts were unstaffed. There was no crossing station on the line, but Dousland was a block post. The speed of trains on this branch was not permitted to exceed 20 mph.

As Yelverton station was 500 ft and Princetown 1,395 ft above sea-level, the line rose 895 ft in a distance of 10 miles 43 chains compared with a direct route of about 6 miles. Passengers travelling over the circuitous line enjoyed (in fine weather) magnificent views from all angles of the Tors of Dartmoor, the valleys of the Meavy, Walkham, Tamar, and Tavy rivers, with Plymouth Sound to the south and the Cornish hills on Bodmin Moor to the west.

The Princetown terminus of the Plymouth & Dartmoor company was further east than the later station; it was located in a garden across the square which afterwards became known as the Railway Arms, and more recently, as the Devil's Elbow Inn.

The Princetown platform at Yelverton in 1933; the branch carriage is 'running round' by gravity, passing the engine tucked in the turntable spur behind.   *R.W. Kidner*

'45XX' class 2-6-2T No. 4591 waits for departure at Yelverton in this 1950s view. *D.R. Kennedy*

Dousland station looking towards Princetown, 3rd March, 1956. *Norman Simmons*

Dousland station from the Princetown end looking towards Yelverton on 3rd March, 1956, the last day of service. *Norman Simmons*

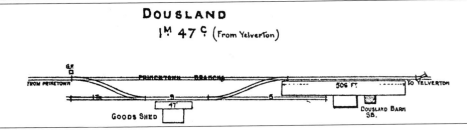

'45XX' class 2-6-2T No. 4568 passing Dousland ground frame and crossing on the 1.22 pm from Yelverton, 31st December, 1955.   *Peter W. Gray*

Burrator and Sheepstor Halt viewed from the train on 3rd March, 1956.   *Norman Simmons*

'45XX' class 2-6-2T No. 4568 arrives at Ingra Tor Halt on the 4.00 pm from Princetown, 31st December, 1955. *Peter W. Gray*

No. 4524 on the 11.20 am from Yelverton soon after leaving Ingra Tor Halt on 2nd March, 1954. Swell Tor Quarry is on the left above the engine. *Top right*, the line can be seen near King Tor Halt. *Peter W. Gray*

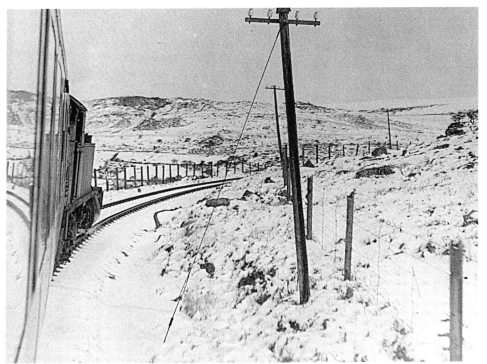

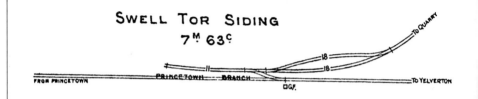

SWELL TOR SIDING
7ᴹ 63ᶜ

FROM PRINCETOWN — PRINCETOWN — BRANCH — TO YELVERTON

OGF.

TO QUARRY

18
18

Left: The Swell Tor Siding ground frame, 31st December, 1955.
Peter W. Gray

SWELL TOR SIDING
GROUND FRAME

Below: Swell Tor Siding with 'Engine Prohibited' notice still *in situ*, 31st December, 1955.
Peter W. Gray

'44XX' class 2-6-2T No. 4401 arrives at Princetown with a mixed train, the 2.28 pm from Yelverton on 11th September, 1953.   *T.G. Wassell*

'45XX' class 2-6-2T No. 4591 arrives at Princetown in this 1950s view.   *D.R. Kennedy Collection*

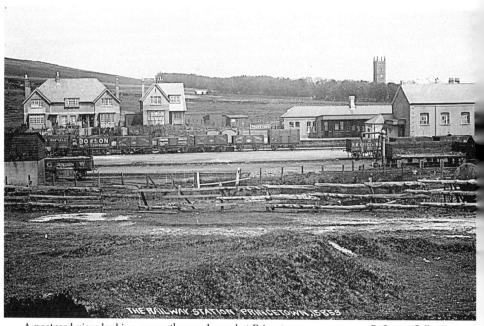

A postcard view looking across the goods yard at Princetown.   *P. Strong Collection*

'45XX' class 2-6-2T No. 4591 stands in readiness for departure to Yelverton in this 1950s view.
D.R. Kennedy Collection

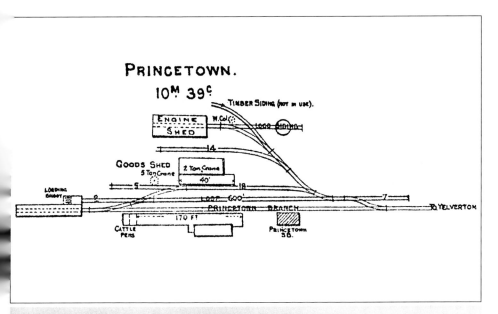

PRINCETOWN.
10ᴹ 39ᶜ

'45XX' class 2-6-2T No. 4530 stands at Princetown in 1954 with the signal box in the background.
Adrian Vaughan Collection

The track layout at Princetown comprised a run-round loop and two parallel goods sidings, one of which was linked, by a crossover arrangement, with the main running line. A third siding served a small engine shed, while a further siding on the south side of the station branched out to serve a timber yard; the latter siding had, however, fallen out of use as early as the 1920s.

There was a single passenger platform on the down side of the running line, and the goods yard was equipped with a goods shed and 40 ft loading platform. The yard crane had a capacity of five tons.

The goods shed, engine shed and station buildings were all built in the standard late-Victorian Great Western style, but these otherwise standard buildings were covered in a drab, grey rendering material that served to accentuate the station's bleak, moorland surroundings. The station building sported a hipped roof and projecting platform canopy, while the single-road engine shed incorporated a water tank in its roof structure.

The station was signalled from a small, two-storey cabin on the down side of the line, and this was equipped with a 14-lever frame. The usual home and starting signals were provided, levers 1 and 14 controlling the up starting and down home signals respectively.

The incline profile of the line shows:

Inclines sleeper than 1 in 200

	Length	Gradient	Falling towards
Yelverton to Dousland	1½ miles	Max. 1 in 40	Yelverton
Dousland station and Lowry Road Level Crossing	2 miles	Max. 1 in 41	Dousland
Lowry Road Level Crossing and 4¼ milepost	½ mile	Max. 1 in 41	Princetown
4¼ milepost and Princetown	6¼ miles	Max. 1 in 41	Yelverton

There were Stop Boards at 11 chains (Princetown) 6 miles 58 chains and at 9 miles 3 chains for up freight trains and at 3 miles 61 chains for down freight trains.

Operating the Branch

There were two block sections on the railway, Yelverton to Dousland and Dousland to Princetown. The line was worked under the electric train staff system. A ground frame at Dousland, electrically locked from the signal box, was attended to by the signalman on duty, while at Swell Tor siding the connection was locked by key on the train staff and attended to by the guard of the train. No down freight trains were permitted to do work at this siding. All trucks for Swell Tor, loaded or empty, had to be taken on to Princetown and returned thence by up freight trains. When necessary the engines were permitted to propel the van back to Princetown instead of going through the section. All shunting had to be done in the sidings; the engine was not allowed beyond the engine stop board at the quarry end of the loop.

At Dousland, a block post, the level crossing was under the signalman's control. At Prowse's crossing there was a gate-keeper, and the gates were interlocked with the signals. At Lowry road crossing where there was neither gate-keeper nor block post, warning bells operated by treadles were in use. Trainmen had to keep a good look-out when approaching and passing the crossing, and in the event of gates being open to the road or the warning bell not ringing, report at the next station, where arrangements would be made for necessary attention to be given. The speed over this crossing was restricted to 10 mph.

Two water cranes were provided at Yelverton, one on the down platform, and one on the Princetown branch line; there was also one crane at the Princetown engine shed.

Turntables, both 23 ft 6 in. diameter, were available on the branch, one at Princetown and the other at the south end of Yelverton station.

The permanent way was worked under the motor trolley system of maintenance with telephones and key boxes fixed at key box No. 1 and at Dousland station and at 7 key boxes between Dousland and Princetown and one at Princetown station.

At the opening in 1883 the following (weekdays only) service operated:

Down		am	am	pm	pm
Plymouth	dep.	8.15	11.20	2.20	5.55
			pm		
Horrabridge	arr.	8.57	12. 4	3. 5	6.37
Horrabridge	dep.	9. 5	12. 8	3.16	6.42
Dousland	dep.	9.16	12.19	3.27	6.53
Princetown	arr.	9.42	12.45	3.53	7.20
Up					
Princetown	dep.	8.12	10.52	2.17	5.42
Dousland	dep.	8.36	11.16	2.41	6. 6
Horrabridge	arr.	8.45	11.25	2.50	6.15
Horrabridge	dep.	8.58	11.31	3. 8	6.25
			pm		
Plymouth	arr.	9.35	12. 5	3.51	7.10

In 1887 the service was five trains each way on weekdays with an additional train on Mondays, Wednesdays and Saturdays, and two trains on Sundays.

By 1910 the train service had increased to seven workings in each direction with two trains extra on Saturdays from Yelverton and five trains with one extra on Saturdays from Princetown. There was no regular Sunday service; this was restored in 1932-3, but withdrawn in later years.

During the summers of the early 1920s an excursion train from Plymouth to Princetown ran on Sundays. The service varied almost from year to year with changes in the number of additional trains run on specified days.

In 1951 there were five down trains including two 'mixed' workings with one additional on Saturdays from Yelverton, and four up trains with two extra on Saturdays and one 'mixed' Tuesdays and Thursdays from Princetown. There was also a freight train on Mondays, Wednesdays and Fridays only, which left

Princetown at 12.55 pm ran to Horrabridge, where it arrived at 2.12 pm and left at 2.30 pm for Yelverton where it formed the 2.51 pm 'mixed' service from Yelverton to Princetown. Wagons loaded with granite were not permitted on 'mixed' trains.

In the early days the line dealt mainly with traffic to and from the prison, together with general traffic for the town and granite from the quarries. During the summer months there was a good deal of tourist traffic.

Prisoners with escort travelled frequently, under special arrangements, until the early 1930s when road transport between the prison and the London & South Western station at Tavistock was used to an increasing extent. During World War II the movement of prisoners reverted to the Princetown branch, but practically all movement by this means had ceased by the early 1950s.

General passenger traffic to Princetown reached its peak in 1931. Goods, minerals and parcels traffic was heaviest in 1903, 1913, and 1923, but declined considerably by 1937 and 1938, by which time the granite quarries were non-producing. Dousland passenger traffic declined seriously after 1931 when the local bus services were introduced.

Snowstorms on Dartmoor were a frequent occurrence during the winter months and there was a standing instruction that when a drift of snow was in prospect, the engine working on the Princetown branch, provided there was an opportunity for doing so, had to be run to and from the threatened spot. Station masters at Princetown and Yelverton had to arrange this according to the end of the branch at which the engine was at the time. If the use of the snow plough became necessary the Locomotive Foreman at Laira and the Control at Plymouth were advised.

Dartmoor winters can be very severe, and it was not uncommon for Princetown to be cut off for days and for the snow plough to be in use to clear the line. The open nature of the country and the high winds which swept around the tors overlooking the railway caused considerable drifting, but fortunately it was not often that a train was snowed up for any considerable period. The worst case was that of the 6.35 pm train from Princetown on 9th March, 1891, which was snowbound for eight days in the Great Blizzard. The train consisted of engine with a composite coach with one first, one second and four third-class compartments. There were two women and four male passengers, with a train crew of three, and five bags of mail.

After leaving Princetown in heavy snow with a high wind, and passing through some large drifts, the train stopped and efforts to shovel away the snow failed. The guard made an effort to reach Dousland for assistance, but was driven back by the weather. A miserable night was spent in the train, which was reached in the morning by three railwaymen who had come from Dousland with food, but the passengers decided to remain in the train rather than attempt the hazardous walk to Dousland.

The next morning they attracted the attention of a farmer rescuing his sheep, but who but who had not seen them because the drift of snow which practically covered the train. They found they were in Eggworthy cutting, near Peek Hill, 5 miles 54 chains from Princetown and 3 miles 23 chains from Dousland. The farmer took them to his homestead and gave them every hospitality. It was not

until 17th March that the line to Yelverton was cleared and it took another day
to finish clearing the line.

Because of the steep inclines and narrow curves, the loads of passenger trains
worked by one engine and one guard was not to exceed six eight-wheel
passenger vehicles. Six-wheel stock was prohibited as was 70 ft stock and
coaches exceeding 9 ft 3 in. wide.

As the engine could not run round its train at Yelverton the following
working was necessary. Upon arrival from Princetown the branch train was
pushed up the line towards Dousland by the branch engine and secured by
hand brakes. The engine then cut off and returned to the platform line, and
stood clear of the siding points which were reversed allowing the engine to
enter the siding. The line was then reset for the platform line and the branch set
dropped by gravity to the platform, when the siding points were set for the
engine to drop back on its train.

In its heyday, excursion trains were run to Dousland on Whitsun and August
Bank Holidays and trains were dealt with as follows:

To avoid the use of two engines on trains between Yelverton and Dousland,
trains requiring assistance between these points were timed to reach Yelverton
to connect with an ordinary branch train. Upon arrival at Yelverton, the
excursion train from Plymouth, the formation of which was not to exceed eight
8-wheel coaches, would draw ahead in the direction of Horrabridge, stand clear
of the branch line points, which would then be reversed, and the train then
steadily backed on to the branch train which had previously drawn up to and
come to a stand at the Yelverton branch starting signal. Both trains were then
coupled, and when this was done, would start together, both enginemen
exchanging signals and starting their engines at the same time.

Upon arrival at Dousland, the combined train would stop with the coaches of
the ordinary branch train at platform, and while passengers were alighting the
branch train was uncoupled by the branch guard, and, as soon as the passengers
had alighted and the train staff handed to the engineman for the onward
journey, the branch train would proceed. The excursion train would then be
slowly propelled to the platform, and after all passengers had alighted the
empty stock would return to Yelverton after the Yelverton-Dousland staff had
been placed in the instrument, and again withdrawn after 'Line Clear' had been
obtained from Yelverton for the empty stock train. Loaded passenger trains
could be banked in the rear from Yelverton to Dousland.

Empty coaches going to Dousland for return excursion trains were dealt with
as outlined above.

Motive Power on the Princetown Branch

The opening of the Princetown Railway necessitated the stabling of some
GWR standard gauge locomotives at Plymouth. The first to arrive were two
single 0-6-0 tanks, Nos. 919 and 923 which had come from the Llynvi & Ogmore
Railway. These were followed by '517' class 0-4-2T engines including Nos. 561
and 563, and by six-coupled tanks of the '1901' class.

No. 4568 on the 2.12 pm from Princetown below Swell Tor Quarry, 31st December, 1955.

Peter W. Gray

For fifty years from 1905 this line was virtually the monopoly of the '44XX' class, Churchward's smallest 2-6-2Ts with 4 ft 1½ in. coupled wheels. No. 3101 came to Princetown in 1905 and the last of the class, No. 4410 left Laira for scrapping in 1955. Between 1905 and 1910 Nos. 3101, 3102, 3103, 3104, 3105, 3107, 3108, 3109 and 3110 all worked on the line, and after the engines had been renumbered in the '44XX' class series from 1912, the other two members of the class, Nos. 4400 and 4406, also appeared on the branch. Their load was 120 tons.

No. 4402 worked the line regularly until 1949. No. 4407 was in evidence in 1952, and No. 4410 from April 1953 to October 1954. The '45XX' class was increasingly used from 1955, No. 4568 being in constant use from January 1956 until the closing day on 3rd March, 1956, and was again seen on the demolition train at Dousland on 15th October, 1956. Engine No. 5567 was seen on 17th November, 1956.

The Closure of the Branch

The closure of the line was not unexpected. Once the main communication with the outside world, the railway was necessary both for the prison establishment and the population of Princetown, but even in its palmiest days, between 1903 and 1923, it is doubtful if it ever paid its way. It is true that its passenger traffic was heaviest in 1931 but during the following years up to the outbreak of war in 1939, all classes of traffic declined.

During the War and up to 1950, it again became a vital link and retained a fair amount of traffic, but by 1955 passengers and goods had dwindled almost to vanishing point. It was obvious that the line had long since fulfilled its purpose and would be one of the first to be considered in connection with the closing of unremunerative lines under the plan for reorganisation and modernisation of British Railways.

Rumours of intended closure began to circulate in 1954, but it was not until a year later that this became certain when staff on the branch were advised that the line might be closed before the end of the year.

The official statement to the public was that the line would stay open until the end of the summer season of 1955, but its future was very much in the air, and unless there was an increased amount of usage it seemed impossible that the branch would continue beyond the end of the year. Local authorities would, of course, be consulted before any action was taken.

It was later anticipated that the line would close on 24th December, 1955, but the eventual closing date was fixed for Saturday 3rd March, 1956.

In the meantime objections were raised by various bodies, the main point being that as Princetown's roads were often impassable because of snow during the winter, the railway should be kept as a means of communication. But as there were at that time no plans for subsidising unremunerative lines on social grounds and because of the improvements in emergency arrangements for dealing with blocked roads, the Ministry of Transport decided in favour of closure.

Several weeks previous to the closing date the traffic on the line was heavy, with family parties and various organisations making their last, and in some cases their first and only journey over the line which had the most magnificent moorland views of any line in the west country, but which was no longer essential to the economy of the district it had served for 73 years.

On the last day hundreds of people travelled over the branch, and Yelverton station staff had the greatest difficulty in finding accommodation for the cars bringing passengers and spectators. The authors are indebted to Eric Shepherd of Plympton for the following account of the closing scenes at Yelverton and Princetown:

Arrived at Yelverton station by car about 2.30 pm. Large numbers of cars outside station. Police on duty parking them, and all available space was soon taken. A large number of people were waiting on the Tavistock platform. The 2.12 pm from Princetown presently drew in with 2-6-2T No. 4568, in reverse (not cleaned up at all), and corridor coaches Nos. 6540, 547, and 7344. Train full. Emptied out and stayed in Princetown platform.

The 2.10 pm from Plymouth then arrived with '45XX' class 2-6-2T No. 4583 in reverse (clean) piloting 0-4-2T No. 1408, with saloon 51 and five coaches. Train full. Engine No. 4583 came off, ran round and coupled up on the other end. The 0-4-2T No. 1408 then took the saloon 51 and the first two coaches, and departed for Tavistock.

Next, 2-6-2T No. 4568 (off the Princetown train) drew out into the tunnel and backed her three coaches onto the three from Plymouth, ran round train and coupled up. People boarded this train for Princetown. Complete train backed into tunnel, drew forward into Princetown platform, where No. 4583 took water.

Train then left for Princetown with following formation: Loco 4568 and loco 4583 and corridor coaches 531, 7359, 2107, 7344, 547 and 6540. Left about 3.25 pm, packed full. Train returned from Princetown, headed by Nos. 4583 and 4568 (both in reverse) about 4.43 pm. Crowded. Stopped at Princetown platform, then pulled into tunnel and reversed onto Tavistock platform. The Princetown locos ran round, backed into tunnel, drew forward to Princetown bay, halted momentarily, then started off for Princetown about 5.15 pm (the 4.51 pm). Train well patronised, but plenty of spare seats.

Drove to Princetown by car, ran into thick mist from the top of Peek Hill onwards. Reached station about 5.45 pm, in high wind, gathering dusk and driving mist. Small crowd on platform and in waiting room: oil and paraffin lights hung up: all windows boarded up and partitions outside 'Gents' end of platform dismantled. Train presently heard whistling and appeared from mist about 5.55 pm.

Got onto train, still plenty of spare seats. Presently locos ran round, train set back short distance into platform and left at approximately 6.12 pm. Few people left on platform: several 'locals' obviously going down and back on train for last trip. Prolonged whistle on leaving, but no detonators or wreaths on locos. (Nor were there any at all during the day.) Police travelled on train. Kept head out of window on right-hand side for most of trip; thick mist and darkness gathering; couldn't see much except dim steamy shapes of two locos nosing around curves ahead and lighted 'serpent' of coaches in front and behind me.

No one at King Tor Halt, but at least one entrained at Ingra Tor. At Burrator two or three people on platform. Train whistled for both level crossings at Dousland and drew into station, where several people were standing, but none got in, then down to Yelverton which we reached on time, at 6.45 pm.

The Princetown train pulled into tunnel and backed into siding by signal box before the Launceston branch train arrived. Princetown train then pulled out of siding, passengers got in, locos took water (which took a long time) and ran round train. Train backed into tunnel, pulled out, and ran non-stop through Princetown platform and so set off for Princetown at 7.30 pm (the 7.0 pm). Small crowd on platform waving goodbye.

Stood in corridor. People waving out of house windows, and people at line-side waving torches; cars ran alongside approaching Dousland, blowing horns and flashing headlights. Small crowd on platform here and cars lined up at level crossing blowing horns and flashing furiously. Stopped at Burrator, but around curve; nobody on platform when we passed.

Two cars under Peek Hill bridge: then we climbed up into mist to Ingra Tor. Saw coaches curving ahead but couldn't hear the locos. At Ingra Tor a voice from rear coach called into blackness 'Is this where I change for Ashburton?'

On to King Tor (no one here) and to Princetown, where saw green of home signal and dim shape of bridge before reaching station. Had to walk up train to alight; crowd on platform; very dark and dismal weather; quite eerie appearance. 'Hostellers' sang *Auld Lang Syne* on platform; few locals here. Locos ran round and disappeared into the mist. (We returned by car to Yelverton.)

The train crews were: Train engine - Driver W. Gough (22 years on the Princetown branch); Fireman, C. Stephens; Assisting engine Driver, F. Coles and Fireman, R. Hext. Guard, K. Gay.

In September 1956 a plan for raising funds to purchase the Princetown line with a view to re-opening was considered by Lydford Parish Council, the authority controlling the Forest of Dartmoor, but this met with little response and the matter was soon dropped.

Although the closure of the Princetown branch was much regretted, local travellers and railway enthusiasts assumed that the 'main line' from Plymouth to Launceston had a relatively secure future as part of the national transport system. Most people regarded railways as a vital part of rural life, and in 1956 it was still thought that the railway network would be retained and modernised. Sadly, this was not in fact the case, and the Launceston branch followed the Princetown route into oblivion in less than six years.

Nos. 4568 and 4583 double-head the 2.15 pm Yelverton to Princetown between Ingra Tor and King Tor Halts on the last day, 3rd March, 1956.   *Peter W. Gray*

'57XX' class 0-6-0PT No. 3686 leaves Ham Green viaduct with the 6.20 pm Plymouth to Launceston train. Bickleigh station can be seen in the distance, 24th June, 1961. *Peter W. Gray*

'45XX' class 2-6-2T No. 4570 approaches Shaugh Bridge with an empty stock working on 4th August, 1962. *Peter W. Gray*

Chapter Ten

The Closure of the Launceston Line

We have seen, in Chapters Seven and Eight, how the Launceston branch was progressively run-down during the years following World War II. At Launceston, for example, the former Great Western station was closed to passengers in 1952, while at Yelverton the signal box was abolished in 1957. These developments were, in some ways, merely the results of improved operating procedures - the closure of Launceston station being a logical step towards greater efficiency in that all passenger traffic was then concentrated in one of the town's two stations.

Closure Proposals

Sadly, the 1960s were a time in which an anti-railway government was keen to promote road transport at the expense of rail, and with the pace of branch line closure speeding up throughout the country, the railway from Plymouth to Launceston fell victim to the government's wildly-swinging axe. The blow came in January 1962 when the British Transport Commission announced that all passenger services would cease between Plymouth, Tavistock South and Launceston, leaving a residual freight-only service between Tavistock and Lifton and at Launceston.

The line had been vulnerable for some time. Its great passenger traffic had fallen off considerably since the early 1950s and much of its freight traffic had been diverted onto other lines. Alternative rail facilities to Tavistock and Launceston were available, although these were already suspect. The Plymouth Corporation and Western National Omnibus Company provided a good joint bus service in the area affected by the proposals.

The usual strong protests against closure were made by public bodies and parliamentary representatives, but the Transport Users' Consultative Committee could not recommend continuation of the services afforded over this section of the Western Region, and the Minister of Transport agreed to closure, to apply as set out below, and with effect from 31st December, 1962.

The sections between Marsh Mills and Tavistock South and between Lifton and Launceston North would be closed completely.

Freight services between Lydford and Lifton and between Lydford and Tavistock South would be operated by the Southern Region, who would also control the goods depot and sidings at Launceston North.

The Last Trains: Ordeal by Snow

It was decided by the Western Region that the scheduled passenger service over the Plymouth-Tavistock-Launceston line should operate on Saturday 29th

The 12.40 pm Tavistock South to Plymouth auto-train crosses Riverford viaduct with '64XX' class 0-6-0PT No. 6438 providing motive power on 20th October, 1962.

Peter W. Gray

'45XX' class 2-6-2T No. 5564 draws into Plymouth North Road from Millbay with empty coaching stock for the 10.40 am to Launceston on 29th December, 1962.   *Peter W. Gray*

Here we see the 10.40 am down service from Plymouth standing at Lifton station on Saturday 29th December, 1962.   *Peter W. Gray*

December, 1962, and that the last trains to use the line would be the 8.35 pm Launceston to Plymouth and the 8.40 pm Plymouth to Launceston.

In the event, these two trains did not run, and the last trains over the line were the 5.40 pm Launceston to Plymouth, the 6.20 pm Plymouth to Launceston, and the 7.10 pm Tavistock to Plymouth workings. This change was brought about by the weather, which had been extremely cold for several days. By the afternoon of Saturday 29th December, 1962 it was evident that Nature was gathering its forces.

It commenced snowing at Plymouth about 3 o'clock, and in the light of what was happening 'up the line' those with responsibility were considering the steps to be taken to meet what might develop into a full scale emergency. Officials, permanent way and signalling department staff off duty were alerted and warned to be in readiness. Traffic and refreshment staff on duty were informed they would possibly have to extend their hours of duty beyond 10 pm to help cope with a situation which was rapidly growing worse.

On the branch line which skirted the southern and western slopes of Dartmoor, the weather became worse about 4 pm but trains were still able to proceed without much delay. Trouble started when the 2.20 pm goods train from Launceston to Tavistock Junction, due to pass Marsh Mills at 4.47 pm was delayed by worsening conditions and could not clear Marsh Mills because of points trouble at the station and at the junction, thus blocking the up line.

The 5.40 pm up service from Launceston to Plymouth, with about 50 passengers, was 15 minutes late in leaving and did not arrive at Marsh Mills until 7.50 pm, 34 minutes late, where it suffered a further delay of about two hours crossing from the down to the up line on account of the freight train being unable to clear. The passenger train eventually arrived at Plymouth at 10.25 pm, three hours late, after further delays between Marsh Mills and Plymouth.

In the meantime, the 6.20 pm train from Plymouth to Launceston, with 67 passengers aboard, drawn by '55XX' 2-6-2T engine No. 5568, left Plymouth 72 minutes late because of the weather and was further delayed thirty minutes between Plymouth and Laira Junction. It was again stopped at Tavistock Junction outer home signal, and Guard M. Crago, Fireman R. Jones and Engineman W. Dornam took turns in carrying out Rule 55 and waiting at the signal telephone for instructions. The line at this point was in very exposed open country by the Plym estuary and the force-10 easterly gale made it difficult for the men to keep on their feet.

After nearly two hours of waiting, the staff at Marsh Mills and Tavistock Junction, by making tremendous efforts, succeeded in clearing the down line. The 6.20 pm train was then able to proceed and reached Marsh Mills at 10.14 pm, 2 hours 42 minutes after leaving Plymouth, and 3 hours 47 minutes late in all.

Meanwhile the 7.10 pm ex-Tavistock, due at Bickleigh at 7.34 pm had to be held at the latter station because of the line occupation at Marsh Mills. The station master, Mr S. Taylor and signalman R. Norris, the only two on duty at Bickleigh, set about clearing and reversing the points at the Yelverton end of the station, and then tackled the task of clearing the points at the Marsh Mills end, preparatory to accepting the 6.20 pm ex-Plymouth. This task it was almost impossible to accomplish; the gale was at its height, the blizzard at its worst. The snow had drifted deeply, the wind blew out the light in the hand lamps, the points were double-ended and by the time they were cleared both men were near exhaustion.

The 6.20 pm ex-Plymouth at Marsh Mills developed vacuum trouble on the last coach which caused further delay, and then made a slow journey on the rising gradient to Bickleigh, which was reached at 11.35 pm, 5 hours 15 minutes late. Three passengers joined the train, but two others from Bickleigh who had gone to Plymouth by the 4.30 pm ex-Tavistock for the 6.20 pm from Plymouth, intending to make the round trip from Bickleigh to Launceston and back, wisely abandoned the idea. After the train crews had changed over the 6.20 pm down service proceeded and arrived at Tavistock South at 12.25 am on Sunday after running through a deep snowdrift near Grenofen tunnel.

Railway telephone communication and the staff token apparatus between Lydford and Tavistock South had broken down, but the Post Office telephone was available and arrangements were made for Pilot working, but this had to be abandoned when the Lydford station master, who was to act as pilotman, failed to reach Tavistock North station when the Southern Region train by which he was travelling was held up by snow near Meldon. The Launceston train at Tavistock South was therefore unable to proceed.

The engine crew were able to maintain steam heating and passengers remained in the train for a while. Meanwhile the station master was arranging for telephone messages to be sent to relatives and friends of the passengers either direct or through the Police Authorities, who rendered valuable service throughout.

About three o'clock in the morning some milk supplies were obtained by the Police, and passengers and railway staff were able to obtain hot tea, using the station office facilities for the purpose. Some passengers were also supplied with sleeping accommodation through the efforts of Civil Defence and the Women's Voluntary Service while others remained in the train or in the station offices.

At about 8 am the station master aroused a cafe proprietor who kindly arranged to supply breakfast. Later in the day, the passengers and the train crew were able to proceed to their respective destinations by road after the snow plough had been at work. The stranded train was brought back to Plymouth on Monday afternoon by a relief engine and train crew.

To return to Bickleigh. An attempt was made to use steam from the engine of the 7.10 pm ex-Tavistock to clear the snow from the points at the Marsh Mills end of the station, but neither engine nor the train could be moved because of frozen brakes. The three passengers and train crew tried to settle down for the night. The station master went to his station house at 1.30 am for rest and refreshment, 'glad to have a "wee drop" from the bottle' having been on continuous duty since 8 am the previous day and without food for 8 hours. Mrs Taylor supplied refreshments to the signalman, the train crew and passengers.

About 2 am the engine ran short of water, and the crew and passengers spent the remainder of the night in the signal box. By morning the snow had ceased, and the Colonel in charge of the Marine Barracks at Bickleigh, having heard

After taking water at Tavistock South No. 5564 on the 12.40 pm Launceston to Plymouth service awaits the arrival of the 12.45 pm down working from Plymouth, 29th December, 1962.

Peter W. Gray

about the stranded train, arranged for breakfast to be supplied, also lunch if required.

About noon a relief engine and crew left Marsh Mills for Bickleigh, but conditions were still so bad that it took about three hours to travel the 3 miles 71 chains. The stranded train left Bickleigh at 4 pm with three additional passengers, who had hiked from Plymouth on the Sunday and called at Bickleigh to enquire for the next train to Plymouth, not knowing that the line had been officially closed on the previous day.

The signalman at Bickleigh had been on duty since 12.30 pm on the Saturday and was glad to sign off on Sunday after he had received the 'train out of section 2-1', signal from Marsh Mills for the 7.10 pm Saturday train from Tavistock.

This epic story of the struggle with the elements is best summed up in his own modest words. 'I had never experienced weather like it. Every time I went out of the box, icicles formed on my eyebrows, ears and hat, and my mac was just a sheet of ice.'

The station master said 'clearing and reversing points in a howling gale and a blizzard, working with the aid of a hand lamp which was continually extinguished by the wind, was exhausting work, and an experience that no one would care to have again.'

The Tavistock station master, Mr R. Hooper, was on continuous duty from 8 am Saturday until late on Sunday, dealing with the situation generally and the requirements of passengers in particular. Signalman H. Maddock was on duty from 2 pm Saturday until after 2 am on Sunday. Permanent way staff who had been called out kept the points clear of snow, and the station master at Lydford, the staff at Marsh Mills and Tavistock Junction, all train crews and staff, not only on the branch but all over the west country, who were on duty at the time, could be proud of the way in which they carried out their task under such trying conditions.

'64XX' class 0-6-0PT No. 6430 leaves Marsh Mills with the 2.10 pm Plymouth-Tavistock South train, 29th December, 1962.   *Peter W. Gray*

Everything possible was done to keep the service going; all gave their utmost, and were defeated only after a tremendous struggle against Nature's forces, to which man, in spite of his cleverness, skill and ingenuity, must ultimately succumb.

Pride in the job, determination and devotion to duty, consideration for and care of the public, these great qualities were never better exemplified than on this occasion, especially when it is considered that despite the running down of their industry, the uncertainty of their future livelihood and prospects, the staff acquitted themselves well; they gave of their best right to the end without thought of personal inconvenience or gain.

The Final Years

The closed line between Launceston and Lifton was re-opened for freight traffic in 1964, but in that same year the southern section of line between Tavistock and Marsh Mills was lifted and the line was closed to all traffic between Tavistock South and Lydford (7th September, 1964).

On 28th February, 1966 the line from Lydford to Launceston was closed, and on and from Monday 3rd October, 1966 Launceston (Southern Region) station was closed to passengers and goods traffic; the last trains through Launceston ran on Saturday 1st October, 1966, and on that sad day the people of this Cornish town lost their last links with the national railway system.

Demolition of the former LSWR and GWR routes was carried out in 1967-68, although some of the abandoned stations remained *in situ* for several years thereafter. Launceston, for example, survived until the early 1970s, but both the Southern and Great Western stations were subsequently demolished to make way for an industrial estate.

Horrabridge station was pulled down to make way for industrial development in 1979, while at Lifton the station site has been engulfed by an enlarged Ambrosia factory.

At Marsh Mills, in contrast, the railway remained in being as a freight-only link for china clay traffic and the Coypool MoD establishment, this residual section of the South Devon & Tavistock line being the only part of the Launceston branch to survive into the 1980s, as part of the BR system.

There had, meanwhile, been further developments at opposite ends of the abandoned route. At Launceston, a 1¼ mile length of 2 ft gauge line was laid on part of the former LSWR route, and in the middle 1980s this short line was operated as a tourist attraction from May to October: there were two steam locomotives and one diesel on the railway in April 1986, though by 1989 this total had increased to four steam engines and two diesel locomotives.

At the southern end of the line, moves were being made towards an eventual re-opening of part of the route northwards from Marsh Mills to Bickleigh. By 1986, the Plym Valley Railway had established an operating base at Marsh Mills and a number of locomotives had been assembled, including six steam engines and one diesel. Within three years, this total had increased to seven steam engines and one diesel, and a length of track had been re-laid on the former trackbed.

Acknowledgements

Grateful thanks are extended to all those who helped Mr Anthony during the preparation of his original book, and to those who have helped in various ways during the preparation of the present volume. Particular thanks are extended to the following.

The Archivist, Devon County Records Office, Exeter
Mr J.R. Hodson, PRO British Rail, Paddington
Messrs F.G. Quant, R. Hooper, E. Kingdom and G. Clark, all of Tavistock
Mr W. Best Harris, Mr Stevens, Mr Baker and Mrs Beckford, of the Plymouth City Library
Messrs A.J. Allen, C.R. Clinker, R.W. Kidner, P.J.T. Reed, A.R. Kingdom, S. Taylor of Yelverton; and Mr S. Taylor and Mr R. Norris, of Bickleigh
Messrs E.R. Shepherd, J.B.G. Ball; M.R. Crago, H.G. Kendall, R.W. Lucas, H.V. Luscombe, J.F. Martin, J.C. Thomas, C. Judge and John M. Strange
Mr R.C. Sambourne for additional research and for permission to reproduce the map of the Marsh Mills area
Mr R.E. Taylor for excellent drawing of maps
Plymouth Railway Circle and Lee Moor Tramway Preservation Society
The Western Morning News
The Illustrated London News

Bibliography

The Plymouth and Devonport Weekly Journal, 1840; *The Plymouth, Devonport and Stonehouse Herald*, 1843-58; *The Plymouth and Devonport Journal*, 1859-62; *The Western Daily Mercury*, 1865-68; *The Western Morning News*, 1865-73; *The South Devon Journal*; *The Tavistock Gazette*

All the above for special and half-yearly reports of meetings.
South Devon Railway, Great Western Railway and London & South Western Railway working tables and appendices.

A GWR half-day excursion ticket.   *John M. Strange Collection*

Further Reading

A.J. Allen	*The Dewerstone*
A.F. Robbins	*Launceston*
R. Burnard	*Dartmoor Pictorial Record*, Vol. II
A.J. Rhodes	*Dartmoor Prison* 1806-1932
H.G. Kendall and	Thomas Tyrwhitt and Princetown
J. Brooking Rowe	(*Report of the Devonshire Association* Vol. XXXVII 1905)
H.G. Kendall	*The Plymouth and Dartmoor Railway*, Oakwood Press
R.M.S. Hall	*The Lee Moor Tramway*, Oakwood Press
T.W.E. Roche	*Plymouth and Launceston*
Sir Harry Ricardo	*Memories and Machines, the Pattern of my life* (James Meadows Rendel)
E. T. MacDermot and C. R. Clinker	*History of the Great Western Railway*, Ian Allan
C.F. Dendy Marshall and R.W. Kidner	*A History of the Southern Railway*, Ian Allan
L.T.C. Rolt	*Isambard Kingdom Brunel*, Longmans, Green & Co. Ltd
J.V. Barron Collins	The Princetown and Launceston Branches of the Great Western Railway, *The Railway Magazine*, Vol. 23 1908 & 24 1909
G.A. Pryer	Princetown, *Railway Modeller*, February 1972
G.A. Pryer	Tavistock South, *Railway Modeller*, March 1972
D. Fenton	Brunel Viaduct in 'N' Gauge, *Railway Modeller*, October 1969
C.J. Freezer	Walkham Viaduct, *Railway Modeller*, October 1969
C.J. Freezer	Locomotives of the GWR: The 45s, *Railway Modeller*, January 1969
Sidney Toy	The Round Castles of Cornwall, *Archaeologia* 1933
T.L. Jones	*Launceston Castle* (1959)
Sabine Baring-Gould	*Devon* (1907)
Arthur Salmon	*Cornwall* (1903)
R.M. Drake-Brockman	Gooch's South Devon Bogie Tanks, *Railway Modeller*, February 1973
Chris Turner	Postwar Tavistock, *Great Western Railway Journal No. 17*, Winter 1996

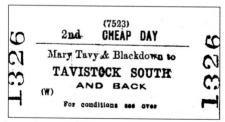

A British Railways cheap day return ticket from Mary Tavy to Tavistock (buff with red 'D' overprint). *John M. Strange Collection*